W9-BVD-008

BEYOND
THE INTERNET

BEYOND
THE INTERNET

HOW EXPERT SYSTEMS WILL
TRULY TRANSFORM BUSINESS

Larry Smith

Copyright © 2001 by Essential Economics Corporation

All rights reserved. No part of this publication may be reproduced
or transmitted in any form or by any means, electronic or mechanical,
including photocopying, recording, or any information storage and retrieval system,
without permission in writing from the publisher.

Published in 2001 by
Stoddart Publishing Co. Limited
895 Don Mills Road, 400-2 Park Centre, Toronto, Canada M3C 1W3
PMB 128, 4500 Witmer Estates, Niagara Falls, New York 14305-1386

www.stoddartpub.com

To order Stoddart books please contact General Distribution Services
In Canada Tel. (416) 213-1919   Fax (416) 213-1917
Email cservice@genpub.com
In the United States Toll-free tel. 1-800-805-1083 Toll-free fax 1-800-481-6207
Email gdsinc@genpub.com

10 9 8 7 6 5 4 3 2 1

National Library of Canada Cataloguing in Publication Data
Smith, Larry W. (Larry Wayne), 1945–
Beyond the Internet: how expert systems will truly transform business
Includes index.
ISBN 0-7737-3327-2
1. Expert systems (Computer science) 2. Business-Data processing. I. Title.
HF5548.2.S64 2001   658'.05633   C2001-901928-9

Publisher Cataloging-in-Publication Data (U.S.)
Smith, Larry.
Beyond the Internet: how expert systems will truly transform business / Larry Smith.
–1st ed. [256] p. : cm.
ISBN 0-7737-3327-2
1. Expert systems (Computer science). 2. Internet. 3. Artificial intelligence. I. Title.
006.33 21   2001   CIP   QA76.76.E95.S63

Cover Design: Angel Guerra
Text Design: Tannice Goddard

THE CANADA COUNCIL | LE CONSEIL DES ARTS
FOR THE ARTS | DU CANADA
SINCE 1957 | DEPUIS 1957

*We acknowledge for their financial support of our
publishing program the Canada Council, the Ontario Arts
Council, and the Government of Canada through the
Book Publishing Industry Development Program (BPIDP).*

Printed and bound in Canada

For my family,
that they may live in a better world

For my students,
that they may see the world they could build

CONTENTS

INTRODUCTION

The image of the Internet is so powerful that it overshadows all of computing. Success on the Internet is assumed to be success in computing. And it is taken for granted that should a single company, like Microsoft, come to dominate the Internet, it would control the very future of computing. Such a fear is groundless.

The Internet is not even new — it's really no more than a souped-up version of the century-old telephone system. Ordering underwear over the telephone is neither especially new nor particularly interesting. Yet both investors and developers remain obsessed with so narrow an opportunity, almost to the exclusion of all else. And the assertion that the Internet is a source of rich profit is, for most companies, absurd.

Cheap communications do not make it easier to do business, they make it easier to *trade*. While auction sites, for example, can lower the cost of a company's components, the overall effect of the Internet is to erode brand loyalty and put downward pressure on the price of whatever the company sells — of whatever most companies sell. When talk gets cheaper, you go from ten competitors to a hundred. This is hardly the way for most companies to make more profit.

The claim that the Internet's ability to mobilize information stands at the heart of business prosperity is equally unpersuasive. It is not clear that providing information to anyone, anywhere, anytime automatically improves either decision making or efficiency. How could it, when this information flow is so vast, chaotic, and corrupted? Information is not made useful or true simply by moving it. If the Internet is the future of business, then business is doomed.

Fortunately, computing is poised to move beyond chat rooms, childish games, balanced accounts, and corrected spelling. A computing technology far more radical than the Internet now approaches. This great family of applications is designed explicitly to aid decision-makers.

Instead of downloading information, these decision-support programs, best called expert systems, deliver solutions. They do so by organizing and verifying knowledge, and by using this embedded knowledge to reorganize work, increase efficiency, reduce waste, and prevent errors. And as human knowledge advances, these effects will be repeated, again and again. Thus expert systems will continuously increase productivity, lower costs, and spur innovation. The world of business will be truly transformed. While the Internet merely helps us talk, expert systems will change the very nature of human work.

In most business environments, computing is used extensively to talk and to "share" information, but it is used only rarely to directly improve decision making. A few will troll through spreadsheets looking for a rule that says, for example, that when inventory falls below a certain level, it is time to add another production shift. Someone else may use "mining" software to discover that customers with VCRs respond better to ads in sports magazines than they do to ads in newspapers. Occasionally, these new rules, limited though they are, may actually be turned into a simple piece of "management" software. Usually, however, the observation resides in a person's head until it is forgotten or ignored in the heat of battle.

The difference that true expert systems will make in the conduct of business is striking. Consider a company that sells equipment to telephone and network operators. Sales begin to rise sharply, and normal decision making plays out all too predictably. The information that now flows across computer screens says sales are up again, and graphs show the increase is far above the historical norms. Memos start popping up on desktops throughout the organization: ship more; make more; hire more workers; raise more capital. Managers surf the Net, clicking on to the news-service headlines that say "telecom is hot" (no reason to read the text: the headline says it all); they also click on to investment sites, and soon notice that their options have made them richer than they were yesterday. Someone sees a snatch of information about a competitor expanding, and another cavalcade of memos follows: hurry; speed product development; hire more engineers; hurry faster. Spreadsheets open by the hundreds, and numbers hurtle from desk to desk. Schedules, plans, budgets roll out, all colour-coded, with exquisite charts and perfect formatting. Production bottlenecks occur. Now the memos exhort action, and all speak with one voice.

Then, within days, sales "suddenly" crash and inventory balloons. Investors panic and stock prices disintegrate. Employees are laid off. This is what happened to Nortel, Lucent, JDS Uniphase, and much of the Internet equipment business. This is exactly what happens when "normal" business practice lags behind the demands of an ever faster, more competitive economy. And the companies' access to the "information resources" of the Internet did not prevent this economic wreckage in the billions of dollars.

With expert systems in place, however, the outcome would have been much improved, the losses minimized. In the first place, the expert systems for information management would have been able to find, sort, and bring into the decision-making process much more external information. In other words, they would have actually forced the use of the information available from the Internet, and equally important, they would have insisted on a diversity of sources and confirmed accuracy. They would, for example, have found repeated warnings from credible sources that all of IT was headed into choppy waters.

The expert systems for marketing would have used no more than the rules available in any good business textbook to advise the managers that the overall economic environment was about to turn hostile. They would have invoked the well-established rule that increasing interest rates slows economic activity, and that this in turn would be enough to push the NASDAQ into a meltdown. The computerized expert would have reminded managers that network operators were buying equipment not from cash flow but from raising capital on the stock market — a process that was about to become much more difficult. In other words, the customers were going to get poorer. In addition, the operators were struggling with the reluctance of their customers to pay for either network access or services. After all, Internet services like e-mail are cheap because supply so overwhelms demand. There is no doubt that the signal from all these expert systems would have been the same: take care; slow down; be cautious; the storm clouds are gathering.

This is most certainly not the power of hindsight. It is *foresight* based on rules that are clearly established and that use information fully in the public domain. Instead of being buried by piecemeal data applied by humans on an ad hoc basis, expert systems bring order and completeness to the search for, and interpretation of, relevant information. The expert systems, of course, can work day and night, monitoring information from a variety of sources and subjecting it to elaborate sets of prioritized rules. Like software programs of the past, they use rules and information, but on a scale exponentially greater in breadth, degree, and synthesis.

Expert systems are able to solve the most complex of problems. They will plan market strategy, advise on acquisitions, and pace product development. Moreover, many of the alleged barriers to expert systems are illusory or incorrect. Scores of business problems, heretofore considered too complex for solution, will fall to the power of computing machinery. As a result, expert systems will invade every aspect of corporate decision making, from marketing to strategy. The speed by which the expert systems will expand their role, and the consequent effects, will leave the marketplace reeling.

A field of battle where the front lines are ever shifting, where norms are overturned and every assumption questioned, where many of the combatants are still fatigued from the Internet wars, holds the conditions for extraordinary victory. Or disaster. The alert will establish the foundations of new commercial empires, or the rejuvenation of old ones, on the high ground that others have mistakenly ignored or abandoned. When all the rules are rewritten, everyone is back at the starting line.

CHAPTER ONE

COMPETITION WITHOUT LIMIT

NOWHERE TO HIDE

On each and every day in the new century, the business executive will wake up and find it more difficult to make a profit, the employee will find it harder to make a living. While each of us sleeps, competitive pressures will be ratcheted upwards because someone else is not sleeping, and thus is gaining on us. No one will be immune, no matter the industry, the technology, or the occupation; no matter whether wealthy or poor, young or old. The furies of competition have been unleashed, and they feed on themselves, growing stronger every day. Turning back this clock will be impossible, though many will try. Others will simply leave the arena.

There is no reason to be surprised to learn that tomorrow's economic hurdles will always be higher than today's. This natural expression of human behaviour has been apparent throughout the centuries. While people are not competitive in all they do, the discontent of humanity constantly pushes us into new terrain, new markets, new products, new ideas — and into the possibilities of what might be. The pioneers are not always right, but they always encounter resistance. From this competitive struggle, new initiatives emerge. Thus slowly, with fits and starts and much backsliding, economic, social, and technological progress unfolds. This is not new.

It could appear new only to those ignorant of history and oblivious to the environment around them. Admittedly, in the past these competitive battles tended to play out in slow motion, with technological advance barely perceptible over the average lifetime. Competitive pressures were no more than glowing embers waiting for fuel. Thus a farmer in the eighteenth century would barely be aware that there had been an advance in agricultural technology. But by the nineteenth century, the next-generation farmer would have seen agricultural practice change significantly. Still, it would have taken a lifetime to do so. In 1900, we should not forget, some farmers in the industrial world were still harvesting grain by beating the stalks with a flail. The design of that flail had not changed since the pharaohs of ancient Egypt held it across their chests as a symbol of authority.

Yet by the beginning of the twentieth century, no one should have failed to notice that the pace of technology was accelerating, driven by that human restlessness that always ends in competitive struggle. Now the car replaces the horse, and a lifetime has only begun. Electricity replaces coal oil, airplanes replace trains, thermal nuclear weapons can end life on earth. And all this happens in *one* lifetime. (But a lifetime is no longer a relevant measure as the pace of change advances.)

This can be seen most easily in the rate at which inventions are adopted into widespread use. W. Michael Cox and Richard Alm established, in their book *Myths of Rich and Poor*, that such inventions as the car, the radio, the telephone, and air travel penetrated the marketplace much more slowly than did the personal computer, the cellphone, or the Internet. Indeed, they suggested that the adoption rate for new technologies continues to accelerate, especially in the information technology (IT) sector. Feeding on its own momentum, competition now revolves in an upwards spiral, the pace and arc growing ever steeper.

It would be easy to dismiss such observations as blindingly obvious. But the real problem is not that popular culture fails to comment on the pace of change — it is that after the change is noted, we all too often go back to business as usual. And those who *think* they are responding appropriately to new technology are many times mistaken. Launching a web site is not even remotely a credible response to the degree of change now demanded.

ADAM SMITH: NEVER MORE ALIVE

Competition will keep growing stronger because there is no obstacle in its path. The number of competing persons, companies, products, and technologies is going to keep rising indefinitely. Competitors are becoming more plentiful for several different but interrelated reasons. For example, many of the legal barriers to competition are falling. Banks can now compete with each other, and with other financial institutions, more freely than before. Trade barriers among countries are also still falling as the World Trade Organization (WTO) continues its work. The practical barriers to enterprise also fall as cheap computing facilitates many administrative and marketing functions. No longer does a business need size to deliver rigorous financial reports or sophisticated marketing materials.

There is also the force of advancing technology itself. It does not just challenge existing companies in a general way. Each new technology is a new competitor in an immediate and direct sense with every other relevant technology. Each new product is another competitor squeezing into an increasingly crowded marketplace. Thus Xerox, for example, is under siege both from competing companies in its previous monopoly domain of electrostatic photocopying *and* from digital imaging technology. Kodak battles the same technology and struggles to defend its market share in old-style film against Fuji. Sears yields to the pressure of

Wal-Mart's superior inventory-control technology. Network television faces declining viewership as eyeballs are attracted by both the Internet and competing cable providers. Home Depot, a new idea in retailing, challenges both malls and downtown shopping outlets, only to be challenged itself by on-line retailing. Yet competitive advantage does not automatically accrue to the new impulse. The dot-coms try a new form of retailing and largely fail, even as they show established retailers a potentially powerful new marketing approach. These advances are, of course, not new; the rate at which they occur is. And they will cease only when imagination fails.

INTERNET: FANNING THE FLAMES

By delivering very cheap communication services, the Internet and its associated technologies dramatically increase competitive pressure. The global capital market, this frantic arena where massive amounts of money whip around the world to capture an extra hundredth of a percentage point, is solely the product of advanced communication. It was possible to move financial capital using the mail, but the slowness of this medium of communication naturally restricted the marketplace. The information lag made trades that were too distant too dangerous. The telephone, especially the cheaper long-distance services made possible by the development of transatlantic submarine cables, steadily improved our ability to place or remove money. As a result, the scope and speed of reaction increased, as did the competitive force of the capital markets. When the Internet drove the cost per message down to almost zero, the global capital market was truly born. Complacent capital no longer had any place to hide.

Indeed, the principal economic effect of the Internet is to intensify every form of competition. It is for this reason that its consequences are rightly described as overwhelming. But as a goldmine of profit, the Internet is most assuredly a questionable endeavour. And it is hard to understand why this is not clearly obvious.

Every advance in communications — from the telegraph and the telephone to the Internet — always adds to competitive pressure. If you cannot talk, you cannot trade, and trading is, of course, the expression of competitive force. Since it is now relatively cheap to communicate with the world, every business needs to do so as soon as possible. Companies must use the Internet to sell, market, and source; otherwise their competitors will do so, gaining the advantage. But because soon every business will be on-line (or will have perished), there is no *abiding* advantage to anyone. The end result is, of course, to make the consumer even more demanding.

Why should I wait for a fifteen-second download? Why did my package get lost as it came to me from ten thousand miles away? Why is your price one-half of a percentage point higher than your competitor's? What have you done new for me today? Why is this brand better than the other? Why should I care about brand, since I am now becoming sophisticated in the use of the Internet? Why do I need a portal at all? In this demanding environment, the Internet *alone* cannot provide handsome profits for most of the businesses that use it.

Not only is the Internet itself cheap, but, as has been commonly observed, much of its content is outright free. Those who have attempted to charge for content have often faced a disastrously low response. Millions of music consumers, for example, have chosen to steal music rather than pay for it. Getting these consumers back in the habit of paying will not be easy, or at least will not produce the profit margins of the past. Eventually, somehow, some way, it is assumed that a revenue model can be worked out for many of these situations. Of course, a *profit* model would be more appropriate, albeit even more difficult. It is amazing what more talk does.

Moreover, even while competitive pressure is visibly growing, the full impact of the Internet has not yet been realized. Most businesses are not even involved in the Internet in a meaningful way, and those that are involved are just starting to realize its communications potential. This means that the number of competitors in actual combat today is far below what it will quickly become. Imagine all the corporations of Europe, China, Latin America, and Japan actually in competition with each other and the enterprises of North America. Then imagine the enterprises of Russia, the rest of Asia, and Africa also involved. The global economy will be real and brutal.

It is important to recognize that competitive combat on the Internet does not necessarily mean e-commerce in the sense that something is actually being ordered or purchased. Indeed, for many companies the nature of their products makes that approach both inappropriate and impractical. But it will be practical and necessary for most enterprises on earth to use the Web as a marketing tool. What is critically important is not whether someone actually executes a transaction on the network, but whether that person learns about your product through the Internet. The Internet must be seen as an extraordinarily powerful, highly flexible, interactive marketing tool. It is the actual forum in which much of tomorrow's competitive frenzy will occur.

The pace of advancing technology and the expansion of the Internet will surely cause a several-fold increase in the number of competing companies, products, and technologies. The only question is how many fold. The response of most businesses today is to manage the next crisis and hope for the best. But the barbarians are gathering at the outer walls, and the sound of fiddling is almost deafening.

CHOICE! EVERYWHERE CHOICE!

This mounting mania of competition, of course, manifests itself in an expanding array of consumer choices. Profit models for tomorrow's economy must without doubt accommodate the increasing range of consumer choice. No matter the business, customers will soon have even more choices than they have today, including choices about who will serve them, at what price, and with which product characteristics. No amount of convoluted logic or outmoded or wishful thinking is going to change that. Unfortunately, ideas that no longer apply are being applied. Amazon.com presents itself as a new response to retailing, but it is actually building brand as if this is 1950 and it is Procter and Gamble. Applying an ineffective tool very aggressively is neither strategy nor innovation.

Business now is much taken by the so-called first-mover advantage.

Get into the market fast and first, then, from a position of dominance, hold your ground. This is supposed to work even if your product is not as effective as those that follow behind. Microsoft is the classic illustration of this argument. It is commonly accepted that Microsoft is not an especially innovative software developer. It invented neither the operating system nor the use of icons. But the phrase "first mover" refers to the mover to the market, not the creator. Microsoft quickly established MS-DOS and Windows as the industry standards. The customer relationship was established, and most important, it became too difficult for the customer to adopt a competitor's "incompatible" product. Added to this weight of habit was the fact that other developers adopted the Windows standard and created further applications. This gave the customer more reason to buy, reinforcing Microsoft's market hold. The result was surging profitability and extraordinary investment returns.

The "lesson" that business learned was the need to rush. This has, of course, produced a spasm of overreaction and ill-considered initiatives of every kind. AT&T reassembles itself and then just as quickly disassembles itself. And tomorrow it shall do something else. Seagram makes liquor, then makes movies, then merges with a utility company to . . . who knows? Disney buys ABC, only to be rescued by the program "Who Wants to Be a Millionaire." Daimler buys Chrysler, and they are doomed to struggle for years into the future.

Of course, the first mover does not always gain advantage, even initially. Ask Netscape. Or ask Pointcast, which was the first mover with so-called push technology and no one cared. But even if the first mover gains some advantage, how should it be sustained? In the olden days, if you had strong barriers to entry, it was possible to endure for a relatively long time. But competition, by its very nature, is about breaching the barriers to entry.

THE GODDESS OF BRANDING

The mantra of the brand is often recited as the white knight that will save us all from the ravages of the Internet. Yet branding is one of the oldest of all marketing tools, the marketing tool with which Procter and Gamble was familiar a century ago. Get to a market first, brand it, and let your competitors try to break the consumer's psychological comfort with you. In the past, that approach worked; however, today branding will serve less and less as a barrier to entry. The rise of the Internet will make this clear; it is true that the Internet changes almost everything.

The effect of the Internet is to increase talk, making each customer more aware of the range of choices and prices. Talk is the enemy of branding. The brand manager does not want the customer to hear some-one else's marketing message. As brands weaken, the defence against competition weakens.

Or are we so overloaded with information, so besieged by advertising, marketing, and messages, that brands will reign supreme as consumers positively flee information? Does a brand offer the consumer the convenience of not having to sort through a bewildering array of infor-mation and information sources? It may seem that it would. And so Amazon.com believes. AOL Time Warner agrees. But they, and many others, are wrong.

They are wrong not because information overload is not a problem. Indeed, it is a problem of extraordinary importance. But that alone does not sustain the argument of the brand builders. While consumers are certainly lazy and creatures of habit, they are also profoundly fickle. They always have been, and it is hard to imagine that they will not be in the future, tempted as they will be with so many more things to be fickle about. In today's world, when so many brands are under siege, consider how many have hardly survived. General Motors' tested and trusted brands have not prevented the long erosion in its market share. Procter and Gamble has some of North America's most powerful brands — or should have, having laboured over them long and hard — yet at this moment, the company struggles to produce more than adequate prof-itability. If brand is such a dominant force, if people are so habit-borne, then network television should still rule the airwaves. In fact it should still *be* the airwaves. If habit is so powerful, how did people find the Internet, seduced as they were away from the powerful brands of the other information media? If brands were so powerful, AT&T would still be top dog in the communication industry.

It is hard to understand an Internet-oriented company extolling the benefits of brand when its very existence is built on having violated the brands of the organizations it defeated or replaced. It is the response of those who have a *single* new idea; on all other issues, they go back to the old tools and believe that they will just execute them more effectively than did Kellogg's or CBS or ABC or NBC or Campbell's or Sears or Control Data or even IBM. Imagine buying a computer called an Apple when Big Blue had carefully crafted its brand image with its enormous weight of resources. Upon this quickly shifting sand, it is hard to see the Internet's long-anticipated treasure-trove of rich and enduring profit.

Amazon.com exists today because it broke the brand connection that Barnes and Noble and thousands of independent bookstores had with their customers. Even though the owners of the independent bookstores were personally known to their customers, "face brand" could not resist the reality of price, convenience, or variety. Yet as Amazon.com develops its technology, it merely demonstrates to everyone else the efficiency of this new form of retailing. With a lag, others then duplicate the innovation. As a result, retail profits remain elusive and transient for all.

The more consumers shop the Internet, the more they can use comparison-shopping tools, and those tools will become ever better. The more they use consumer decision-support tools, the more brand is weakened. The more shopping is automated, the more brand is weakened. If you can shop on-line, why would you ever go to only one place when the next place, instead of being across the city in a snowstorm, is simply a keystroke away? And if consumers hesitate as they mount the learning curve, it is merely the lull before the storm.

In the beginning, a pioneering information technology will attract those who want the newest and the coolest. These "first-mover customers" will flock to Netscape, Yahoo, or eBay. If the seller can say, "This is cool, and I shall hold your hand," then the second wave of customers will arrive. Thus AOL grows. Yet both strategies are inherently self-extinguishing. As AOL's customers become accustomed to the

Internet, they no longer need their hands held. And those whose hands have been held will then turn into idiosyncratic teenagers who flee home as quickly as they can. If all you had to do in the new age of competition was create an image of a comfortable old friend, then IBM would still be the colossus that bestrides the computer industry. However, this approach — trying to be all things to all customers in the safe and comfortable middle road — ultimately did not work for IBM. Finally, it was no longer enough to run one's business on the assumption that no one ever got fired ordering IBM's products. Thus IBM wanders in the wilderness, comfortable turned into stodgy. Its brand is doing no more than keeping it alive.

The surest sign that business consultants and commentators have become desperate in their attempts to stave off the logical consequences of competition (perhaps so as not to annoy clients) is that they advance the "last man standing" argument. This so-called strategy describes the company that has deep enough pockets or patient and gullible enough investors to allow it to outbleed its other competitors, until it is the last man standing. However, there is no assurance that the last man can remain profitable in an industry that has no true barriers to entry besides threat. If the "last man" company actually does then enjoy high profit, competitors will return, this time probably wiser and better funded. There is, as the markets have proved again and again, no shortage of suicide capital.

In spite of how sophisticated the marketing argument becomes, or the numbers of diagrams drawn and slogans reiterated, the basic effect of the Internet is described by the evocative word "disintermediation." The logic is elemental. By facilitating communication, the Internet reduces your need to have someone talk on your behalf, mediate on your behalf (that is, you need not talk to the store owner, who talks to the local wholesaler, who talks to the regional distributor, who talks to the importer, who talks to the producer). As the talk, and the desire to buy, proceeds from company to company, and as the goods and services return from company to company on their way to the final customer, the process slows, the inventory balloons, and the costs naturally rise. So, of course, does the likelihood of error.

The telephone is itself a spur to disintermediation. All across North America, newly established call centres are manned by hundreds of agents receiving customer complaints, queries, and orders. A short time ago, these functions would have been handled by the merchant or the distributor. Now part of the distribution process is being pulled back to the original producer. Instead of talking to the grocer, for example, a customer who suffers a cookie emergency is able to call the cookie hotline.

The rise of the discount broker clearly shows the power of communication to circumvent normal distribution channels. The old model involved a personal investment adviser-cum-gatekeeper who provided recommendations and executed trades. Naturally, this produced handsome commissions in a staid and predictable business. Then the discount broker arrives and dispenses with advice. Trades are executed by phone for much lower fees, and the brokerage business changes forever.

The number of discount brokers proliferated, and the Internet accelerated the process as on-line trading became practical. Now the discount customer is able to download more advice and information than the human adviser could ever have delivered. The downward pressure on fees remains intense.

Appropriately enough, the distribution of computers themselves was dramatically affected. Michael Dell decided that personal computers were no longer so new or intimidating that they needed the services of a retailer. So Dell Computer specializes in selling directly to the customer, eliminating an entire link in the distribution chain. Again, the phone played a part, and the Internet quickly made the process cheaper and easier for both the customer and Dell. As a result, the widespread adoption of the personal computer accelerated and competitive pressure was ratcheted upwards.

In general, the Internet reduces the number of links in the distribution chain between the producer and the final customer. And as that chain shortens, competition rises because the number of competitors also rises. Instead of buying its goods from four distributors, a store can now buy from two thousand manufacturers. The wholesaler's bottleneck is broken, and war is waged much nearer the final buyer. Of course, for many goods and for very many services, the store becomes ultimately unnecessary. There is no mediation at all between the producer and the customer, as they both use the Internet to talk directly to each other.

Even though disintermediation is already visibly under way, as Dell makes quite clear, the response of many companies yet again is to believe that tomorrow is only going to be a little bit different from today. They therefore propose to deal with somewhat less mediation without preparing in a meaningful way for the future. Of course, disintermediation will take time, and it will not apply to every product and every market. Yet the direction of change is clear and the speed of adoption for any innovation is faster than was true in the past, precisely because of rising competition. Therefore, while these changes will certainly be phased in, it is wholly inadequate to try to muddle through with no strategy other than to rush into the comforting arms of the goddess of branding.

The point is not that brands never work. Of course they do, and when carefully nurtured, they can command premium prices and profits. But they have never been able to resist a significant innovation. They did not protect ships from planes or typewriters from word processing. The very best branding can do is slow the rate at which an innovation is adopted. This would give the established players time to create their own imaginative response. However, all too often these players create only a new advertising campaign. Thus Xerox nurtured the photocopier while the colour printer redefined the marketplace. The worst situation occurs when the brand does not fail outright, but merely produces marginal profit. Years will then be wasted in the vain attempt to "tinker" it back to its glory days.

Companies can be partly forgiven for missing the weakening effect of branding. In the past, brands were stronger because brand-busting innovations were introduced much more slowly. It was the slower pace of technological advance that allowed brands to thrive. Since much more of the competition was among established brands (rather than actually new against actually old), it was natural for companies to use every conceivable branding gambit in order to gain a tenth of a percentage increase in market share. And as always, the responses of the past imperil us today.

Unfortunately, when branding obviously and finally fails, too many companies then create strategy by throwing ideas against a wall to see if they will stick. A little more sophistication for the age of information seems appropriate. The telecom networks, for example, their century-old brand value apparently exhausted, now plan to deal with the explosion of communication choices by selling content, even though they have no experience in either selling or creating content. And there is no particular reason why the producers of content, with so many choices of distribution available to them, should share with the networks anything more than a modest distribution fee. Yet it is upon this strategy that some networks base their return to profitability (or at least a semblance of profit).

As more competition creates more customer choice, more choice just as inevitably shifts power to the consumer from the producer. But while it may be obvious, this fact often does not elicit a response. Even while offering more choices to their consumers, many companies still fail to see this as a direct assault on their profitability — or at least they do not see it as a significant enough threat to induce a thoughtful reply to the challenge. The Internet fundamentally increases choice, and brands ask customers to abstain from choice. The Internet cannot serve both purposes. If a company embraces the Internet, it is embracing choice, and it had better be prepared for the consequences.

WHY BIGGER IS WEAKER

From the beginning, AOL worked aggressively to build its brand. Nevertheless, it is a compliment to AOL's management that they saw their vulnerability and used their exceptional stock value to merge with Time Warner. Time Warner also saw the threat to its venerable brands — brands that were producing far from handsome profits. It is significant that CNN, Time Warner's icon brand for new media, is suffering falling viewership, and that its web sites are far from overwhelmingly successful. As is often the case, the weaknesses that bring merger parties together often become strengths during the merger press conferences. Thus AOL and Time Warner extol their stable of powerfully established brands, synergistically reinforcing each other. While it is possible for brands to prop each other up, AOL Time Warner has its other great problem to overcome.

Of the strategies to deal with the erosion of market power, the pursuit of greater size through merger and acquisition is surely the strangest. Both AOL and Time Warner cited the speed of technology as one of the reasons they joined together. They got bigger to deal with rapidly changing technology, even though as they increase in size, their decision-making ability inevitably slows. With decision making moving more slowly, the response to changing technology, and to the new market opportunities that arise from the technology, is slowed. Increasing size and faster response are incompatible, plain and simple.

There are undoubtedly advantages to size, of course. There are the weight of resources, the depth of talent, the borrowing capability, and the encouragement and support of investors. And more resources mean that the larger organization can run experiments and survive their failures, a necessary path to innovation. Once a decision is made, a large organization can bring much effort to bear. But the ability to respond with supporting resources is an advantage only after the decision to commit has been made. And that is exactly the problem. Bigger inevitably means slower with respect to the key ingredient of decision making, a deadly attribute in an economy moving, as they say, at Internet speed.

The bigger you are, the more you have to talk to yourself. There are more people in the organization to talk to, more people to coordinate with, more people making sure that other people are not out of control and that financial targets are met. There is more reporting, consultation, and feedback. Talking is inevitably slow, and there is no technological solution yet that speeds up this process. Of course, dominant technologies like e-mail or shareware actually increase the generation of talk. Sharing information about the prey while riding a herd of tigers is as awkward an idea as it sounds.

The new IT technologies do not speed the generation of decisions, no matter what Bill Gates would have us believe. How could information overload possibly cause decisions to be made more quickly? In fact, the only way it could accelerate decision making is if it required the recipient to ignore much of the information available, and thus make decisions arbitrarily (that is, with whatever is presently in the decision-maker's head). Thoughtless decisions made in the swirling complexity of today's economy are an invitation to disaster.

Many of the recent mergers and acquisitions in information technology are justified on the basis of the synergy involved in cross-selling and promotion. But that merely increases the amount of liaison and consultation that must occur. Instead of merely having to talk with those within your corporate department, you must now have marketing in the music subsidiary talk to marketing in the cable subsidiary. This greater volume of talk must now occur across institutional barriers and with persons who are greatly tempted to defend their independence of action by talking endlessly. Time Warner was susceptible to what well appears to have been a takeover by AOL because the company was not particularly profitable in comparison with AOL. This was in spite of the fact that the merger of Time and Warner was supposed to create synergistic bliss. As was the combination of Disney and ABC. As was the combination of Daimler and Chrysler.

Whatever the answer to the punishing increase in competitive pressures, it will not be found in the growing size of enterprises, at least as traditionally organized and equipped. Such organizations will be slower rather than faster, and slowness in the domain of accelerating technology cannot be the path to success and profitability. The pursuit of sheer size is the corporate strategy of a century ago. It is ironic indeed that many of those who worship at the altar of IT also appear enamoured of the alleged benefits of size.

There is an ultimate answer to the pressure of rising competition, an answer that involves a different kind of organization and a different set of tools. Ironically, this alternative can accommodate both reasonable size and speed, where size is a natural by-product of market success, not a defensive response. This answer lies in a different domain, however, and threatens the dinosaurs. The answer is not merely to use IT in some vague and general way.

THE RATE OF RETURN UNDER SIEGE

As competitive pressures rise, there is inevitable downward pressure on profitability. As you shift power from the producer to the consumer, the power you shift is the power of price. It becomes harder to extract the price that produces a high profit, and therefore a high rate of return. And even though this shift is proceeding relatively slowly, the stress on profitability is inevitable.

Overall trends in the economy can obscure this long-run pressure on profits. When interest rates are high, profitability falls. When interest rates fall, profitability rises. But in the latter case, profitability is rising solely because it is no longer being crowded out by higher interest rates. That is not the same thing as a systemic increase in profitability. Thus the increase in profitability in the early 1990s was the natural response of the system as the abnormally high interest rates of the past returned to their historic levels.

The best way to judge corporate profitability is as its share of the national income stream — that is, as a percentage of gross domestic product (GDP). And by this most basic measurement, the economy of the United States did not experience rising corporate profitability in the latter part of the 1990s. Since 1996, the proportion of GDP going to corporate profits has been relatively stable, at just under 10 percent. This profit plateau occurred even as the U.S. economy enjoyed exceptional growth and strong consumer demand. That fact alone was a clear warning sign to the stock market as it started factoring in extraordinary future profits.

In Canada, by contrast, corporate profit as a share of GDP rose in the latter 1990s to about 12 percent. However, corporate profits are historically higher in Canada than they are in the United States, and this increase merely took the Canadian performance back to its historic norm. Again, there was no sign of profit breaking out of its normal range, even as the stock market broke out of its normal range.

Moreover, the total share of U.S. GDP going to corporate profit and interest income together remained relatively stable, as did the share accruing to wage earners. Employee salaries and wages constituted between 46 to 48 percent of GDP during the 1990s, rising slightly towards the end of the decade. In other words, against the backdrop of a competitive marketplace, the rewards of economic activity continued to be divided relatively evenly between employees and the owners of corporate capital. This means, of course, that the competitive marketplace was rewarding the fact that the productivity of the worker was rising at least at the same rate as the worker's endowment of tools, plant, machinery, and equipment (that is, the value of the human capital embodied in the worker's education, experience, and expertise balanced the growth of physical capital). With all this capital investment, the investor has reaped a return that stays just abreast of the reward of the worker. Wall Street is not so powerful as its investors suppose, since all it does is protect the owners of capital from falling behind. This occurs, of course, because the financial markets are highly competitive, in an economy that is becoming more competitive.

In addition, the quality of the profits themselves is deteriorating. A rapidly changing economy with a rapidly changing technology, paced by accelerating competition, must inevitably produce highly volatile profits — a volatility that, if it is going to do anything, is more likely to grow than to diminish. Since all investment is inherently a commitment to the future, the uncertainty arising from this volatility represents a serious obstacle to the ability to raise capital. In the face of this uncertainty, the natural response of investors is to seek short-term opportunities; thus in the highly competitive situation we face, and will continue to face, patient capital becomes a scarcer and scarcer commodity.

Unfortunately, without long-term patient capital, enterprise cannot undertake long-term initiatives. And without long-term initiatives, a company cannot have sustained competitive advantage. As a result, enterprise runs faster and faster to stay in the same place, unable to extricate itself from the dead end in which it and its investors now find themselves.

Of course, it was easy to finance a dot-com. They were all expected to go public quickly and give the investor a rapid exit. (Business plans, of course, always reflect the latest fad, and thus there was often more documentation about the "exit strategy" than the "build it up" strategy.) Yet hundreds of excellent investment opportunities, outside of e-commerce, lay fallow because investors might have had to wait a whole two years before they could take their capital and run. That is not a foundation on which we will be able to build commanding advances in computing or in any other kind of technology. Of course, the base technology that drives computing and the Internet was not created by capital that would commit itself only for short periods of time. But now, apparently, the only advances are those that can be sustained over the course of the next couple of months.

CAT ON A HOT TIN ROOF

Startlingly enough, even though impatient capital is the curse of long-term growth, many business commentators have chosen not to reiterate the old virtues. They have chosen not to call attention to this self-defeating orientation of investors and managers. Rather they have, yet again, invented a new set of buzzwords, the best defence against thought. Some speak of "agile management" as a logical response to the frenzy of the real and the financial marketplaces. In other words, management sits poised and watchful, ready to rush in and duplicate any idea that appears to have proved itself. Companies are supposed to sweep aside the first mover and use massive resources to take a commanding position. Of course, the agile do not actually create anything; they are merely supposed to dominate the creations of others. Their only skills are that they are alert and big and can move quickly, even though being big and moving quickly is a contradiction in terms. The logic of agile management is simply a rationalization of what is happening, not a formula for getting off the competitive treadmill. Agile management will never create any substantive technological advance, or contribute anything of high value to the customer. But it always seems better to join the herd and cry, "Forward, forward," than to say, "There is a great turning ahead."

Yet trendy is as trendy does. Everyone tries to be agile, and Silicon Valley's workers jump from company to company at an ever faster pace with an ever fatter signing bonus. And let no company decry that labour mobility, not when it practises the same strategy. A firm has little moral high ground from which to criticize its workers for being agile when its own attention span is measured in months rather than years.

When Alan Greenspan, head of the Federal Reserve Board, announced that he would cause the economy of the United States to slow, a capability that is well within his and his institution's power, we should have remembered all the learned commentators who calmly and confidently proclaimed that an economic downturn would not affect the blessed domain of technology, and certainly not the IT empires. It does not matter if interest rates rise, said the cheerleaders, because the IT industry does not trouble itself with borrowing. Investors are so enamoured of IT, so oblivious to the lack of profit, that they will give it equity no matter what else is happening in the economy. No matter the volatility of earnings, no matter the absence of earnings — no matter any of this — the money will still flow. This argument is not silly in retrospect — it was silly when it was spoken. It was silly *before* it was spoken, because it was not supported by any economic experience or common-sense logic. The profits of IT companies, of course, fell as the economies of the United States and much of the rest of the industrial world slowed. And as the profits fell, so did IT stock prices.

It could not have been any different, given the aggressiveness with which the computing industry has rushed into the particularly volatile consumer and retail market. Let us sell more toys to big children instead of productivity tools to business because . . . Because there are more consumers than businesses? Because retail consumers are more stable customers? Because the toy market is so wonderfully stable? Every *experienced* toy maker on earth knows that toys have always been a most fickle product category.

With the economy now slowed, profits eroded, and the stock markets down (the NASDAQ *sharply* down), the supply of capital for new ventures has dramatically fallen. Capital from initial public offerings (IPOs) and venture capital companies is scarce. Now even impatient capital has taken flight. But there is little sign investors now understand that perhaps they should fund longer-term, aggressive IT possibilities, ones that will feed into the long-term needs of the marketplace instead of its transient impulse to buy a new video game with a really cool helmet. If they do not flee to the other extreme — fixed-income securities — investors buy big on the assumption that big is secure. Or they stand on the street corner looking sad and confused.

The slowdown of the North American economies has produced no small amount of wreckage. The dot-coms became the dot-bombs, as dozens fell on the battlefield, from Boo.com to eToys. Yahoo stumbled and its stock tanked. Dell, Cisco, and Nortel have laid off thousands, as has the brokerage industry. The auto industry slows sharply, and the telecommunications sector acts as if it is shell-shocked. Unfortunately, too many large, well-funded organizations improvised their way forward, bobbing and weaving furiously as they sought something profitable to do in some vague set of circumstances. That this all came undone with the slightest blast of cold economic reality is unsurprising. But what else could we have done? the proponents of agility ask. Since technology moves so quickly, what choice is there but to become Don Quixote and charge off to an unknown destination?

The most common excuse for this lack of focus is the argument that the future is unknowable. It is the great justification for every ill-considered, unplanned, precipitous, and foolish act that has ever occurred. If you cannot understand the future, you need not take responsibility for anything more than the next several minutes, and without responsibility or accountability, you have no need for a plan. Many companies plan in exquisite detail the most trivial matters while leaving the largest elements wholly up to fate. The argument that the future is unknowable is itself an argument of ignorance. It is to say that we do not know what happens to the pace of the economy when interest rates rise, do not know what happens to equity values when profit falls, do not know the reaction of customers to low quality in the long run, and do not know what happens as competitive pressures rise.

This is to say we could not have imagined the impact as high-quality, inexpensively priced Japanese cars arrived in North America. Who could have foreseen that such a development would cause the erosion of the market share of the existing auto industry? How could we have imagined that if companies offered very cheap mobile telephone service, millions of people would take advantage of it? How could we have imagined that people would stream onto the Internet to use e-mail, simply because it was so cheap? Who could have known that volume would rise because communication was so inexpensive as to be negligible? Who could have known that rising volume would create a premium demand for the technology that increased the network capacity? Who could have known that somebody must pay for the network infrastructure?

Who could have known that in the early days of a transforming technology, a gold-rush mentality would cause the great telecommunications networks and their suppliers to tremble within the shadow of an economic meltdown? Who could have known that some of the great networks are simply retelling the early days of the railways? Who could have known these things in advance? The student of history would have known. The student of logic would have known. A thoughtful person would have known.

The lack of long-term focus is the same thing as the lack of strategy, since by definition a strategy must be long term. And that certainly means more than a year; everything else is tactics. The real issue for any value investor is not whether a company can be profitable tomorrow but how high its profits will go and how long they will stay high. It is all too telling that much of the commentary about the profit of companies in the IT sector emphasizes their immediate profit and almost never their long-term profitability. In spite of all the talk about the importance of price-earnings ratios with respect to future earnings, the analysts' expectations remain focused on the next several quarters.

The lofty price-earnings ratios of much of the IT industry could be justified only by the most extraordinary *continued* increase in profits. Yet rare is the analyst who will actually give a number to that presupposed extraordinary increase in profitability. Often price-earnings ratios are based on the belief that profits will be huge. And "huge" is as precise as the observation gets. Should you press an analyst on this point, you will likely be greeted with the old answer that technology and the marketplace move too quickly to be any more precise. This approach is of hardly any value to the portfolio managers of the great capital pools, whose responsibility to their shareholders or claimants extends far into the future. While this lack of long-term focus affects the IT industry to a particular degree, it is common throughout the entire business community.

THE POWER OF THE AVERAGE

To the student of history, the long-term profitability of any particular enterprise reverts to the mean.[1] This chilling observation says no less than that even a highly profitable company will, over time, tend to approach the industry average. In other words, the high flyers become average flyers over time. The list of the mighty that have descended to mortal status is long indeed: Control Data, Westinghouse, Sunbeam, Xerox, Kellogg's, Procter and Gamble, Boeing, AT&T, Kmart, CBS, NBC, RCA, Sears, Kodak, and many others. The phenomenon is present in all industries, and some of these companies passed the industry average only as they fell below it.

The most compelling of all such examples is IBM. In its heyday, IBM made more money than all its competitors combined. It successfully evolved from business machinery into computing machinery, and by understanding the market better than its competitors, it pushed computing into the mainstream of business. If any company had long-term

---

1 Eugene F. Fama and Kenneth R. French, "Forecasting Profitability and Earnings," *Journal of Business* (April 2000).

momentum, a deep pool of talent, and market dominance, it was IBM. Nevertheless, today it produces utility-like returns and lumbers along in the shadow of other computing companies.

Yet this argument suggests that underperforming companies revert to the average as well. This may be as much a self-selection process as anything else, however. If underperforming companies do not return to the industry average, they will be starved of capital and fade away; it is also possible that those that are underperforming are under severe pressure to focus on critically overdue responses.

The honour roll of companies that have recaptured their former glory is long enough to give courage to all those who struggle, including the poor investor. Disney advanced under Walt, faded under his successor, and took off again under Michael Eisner. And now it battles to regain its lost momentum. General Electric threatened to become an average company until Jack Welch spent a decade turning it into one of the world's great success stories. The Ford Motor Company is surely the comeback kid of all time. As a founding member of the automobile industry, it enjoyed explosive growth by selling cheap cars for the mass market. Yet after the Second World War, the company almost collapsed, only to rescue itself with professional management and innovative designs like the original Mustang. It then faded under the assault of Japanese imports. But again, it regained its momentum and now leaves General Motors and DaimlerChrysler struggling in its wake.

High flyers revert to the average because competitors enter the marketplace, because they grow too large to respond, or because they have a single idea and cannot produce a second. That second idea might, of course, have been just one millimetre outside their line of vision. Kodak was unable to imagine the value of electrostatic photocopying, even though in the early days it could have acquired it. Nor did the company recognize the potential of instant photography, which was even closer to its domain of interest. That is one example of many where the next industry innovation did not arise from the dominant player.

THROUGH THE LOOKING-GLASS CLEARLY

The key question is not whether assured high profitability would be a good thing, but whether it could be dependently anticipated in an economic universe where all profit seems illusory, where it's easily swept aside by one quarter's or one year's worth of difficulty. But there is a way to create assured long-term profit even in the midst of disruptive technical and marketplace change, an old answer that explains how to create long-term value. An answer that Adam Smith understood.

There is nothing about this solution that is either in question or surprising. High long-term profit is achieved when you deliver to the customer a premium-value product that the customer will need for the next hundred years. You will make sure that the product works effectively and efficiently, and you will make it better every year. The pharmaceutical industry is the classic illustration of this. If it chooses the right line of research, it can sell health and sometimes life itself. As long as it is able to do so, its profits remain high. And it is hard to imagine circumstances in which its services will no longer be needed.

Xerox was once in such a situation, making handsome profits by selling the ability to replicate information more effectively and cheaply than the alternative. Again, there was no plausible reason to expect the *need* to replicate information to disappear. Unfortunately, Xerox forgot it had to make its product better every year. So it missed laser printers and the advent of digital reproduction. Now it must play catch-up. Disney, although struggling to improve itself, built an empire on the idea that families will *always* want to have fun together.

You can create such a dominant position by choosing a market need that others ignore, whether the need is to lower blood pressure, improve mail service, or entertain families in a park-like setting. In the ultimate manifestation of this strategy, you are the only one who knows how to satisfy that need. This is the strategy for the information age. It is beyond the infrastructure of the Internet. It is about mobilizing information to high purpose in a way that only you can. This simple and straightforward idea is the foundation on which computing's next great empires shall be built.

Listen to the echoing cries of objection, and that alone will tell you the strategy is correct. The critics will say the goal is impossible, except in the rarest of circumstances. But how many times has opportunity been lost in the glib assumption of impossibility? How can we look back on the previous century and ever easily issue the accusatory word "impossible"? Most things once thought impossible will, upon examination, appear only to be very difficult.

The critics ask how it's possible to pursue such a long-term strategy. How can anyone ever be sure about what people will need far into the future? How can you be sure of your solution when technology changes so quickly? How can you anticipate aggressive technological change? Interestingly enough, that particular question is irrelevant. We need only predict the demand conditions that arise from the most fundamentally unchanging characteristics of the marketplace. What the marketplace does now is what it did five thousand years ago; what drove the market then drives it now. An IT professional can claim otherwise only if he has never looked beyond the ghostly images on his computer screen.

We cannot predict when technological innovations will happen — and in some cases, even if they will happen — but it does not matter. When innovators know what demand to pursue, they use *today's* technology to create a solution. That is particularly easy if today's technology is not fully used. Moreover, if you focus on the market needs that are being disregarded, the odds of finding a technology that is available but underused are very high.

The most startling illustration of this approach destabilized the U.S.-based automobile industry and continues to put it under competitive pressure. The Japanese automakers became persuaded that quality could be dramatically improved by following the suggestions of America's leading advocate of rigorous quality control, W. Edwards Deming. They then adapted existing automobile technology to create technically superior vehicles, much to the delight of consumers. That level of quality had not been available before because U.S. automakers had, as a corporate policy, chosen not to use existing technology to that end. Of course, the reason the Japanese could make such significant progress was that so much technology to improve quality was already available. This technology included, among other elements, advances made possible by the U.S. space program and computer-based just-in-time (JIT) inventory controls.

The next logical step is to use the resources of commercial success to create further advances in technology. While this approach applies to any market demand, it is of exceptional relevance to the IT industry. It is IT that has an abundance of unused technology, and that particularly invites the creation of new products and offers an extraordinary potential for proprietary technology. For example, computer-based learning has long been available in basic form. Yet its use in most schools is no more than peripheral. Web page design tools are well developed, but many web pages are baffling. Computer security programs could guard corporate secrets, but they are not fully employed. Business databases could hold real corporate histories, and they do not.

This approach requires imagination rather than superficial impulses or aggressive imitation. Unfortunately, most people assume they or their organizations are capable of no more than imitation or reaction. Too many people believe that it is impossible (that word again) for them to be truly creative. That, they believe, is the domain of the guru sitting on the mountaintop and getting light headed from the lack of oxygen. This is the second greatest excuse for lack of thought and ambition.

Fortunately, those who follow a more imaginative approach will be in the advantageous position of having few competitors — a benefit in the marketplace that is difficult to overstate. Imagination is such a last resort that it will be entertained only when the economy is calm or becalmed. When next the NASDAQ rises, the herd will again plunge forward with reckless enthusiasm. Value investing will fade again, and agile management will have its second wind. The bio-technological bubble will erupt several times in several different manifestations, since it is "surely" the next big thing. Like all "next big things," it will lose as much money as it makes, mislead as many people as it gives guidance to. The tendency of the herd to run crazy and then pause in fright, only to run wildly in yet a new direction, will continue for some time yet. But eventually a much more profitable approach will triumph. And that approach will be centred on information in its highest expression.

THE DEMAND OF THE NEXT HUNDRED YEARS

The market that produces the most assured profits is the market whose demand is most stable, whose demand is the same today as it will be in 2101. This is the market that provides technology to the business sector; it is one of the planet's oldest markets, and no acronym — not even B2B — can make it new.

We know what the businesses of 2101 will want — it is what they want today. They will want to sell more. They will want to lower costs. They will want to make more profit. Give them the tools and the conditions to do so, and they will buy your product.

And the only significant difference between today and 2101 is that the future desire to sell more, to lower costs, and to make more profit will be many times more intense than it is today, a direct consequence of relentlessly rising competitive pressures. This demand weakens only when competitive pressures abate, which they most assuredly are not likely to do. Growing economies merely stimulate more technological change, which itself adds to the competitive pressure to innovate. And when the economy weakens, the need to preserve eroding profit grows intense. So whether you need to become more effective to avoid being left behind or to maintain profit to avoid destruction in an abating field of enterprise, the demand for profit tools rises.

It is equally certain that demand will outstrip supply. Demand for unique profit tools is essentially open-ended, since you can never be too profitable and since today's profit is always under the threat of tomorrow's competition. But by contrast, the supply of such unique profit tools is always fixed at a point in time.

Increasing the supply of new profit tools is an exercise in imagination, as is the case for all significant innovation. Since imagination has been in short supply from the beginning of time, and since contemporary society has not yet made any systematic attempt to nurture this skill, the supply of innovation lags its demand. In addition, the IT industry, the most fertile ground for most profit tools, continues to undervalue this market need.

This is not to argue that the consumer market is of minor consequence, but it is a much more complex, wildly competitive marketplace. The demands of the consumer are extraordinarily difficult to anticipate. It can truly be impossible to understand why someone prefers french-fried potatoes to french-fried turnips, why a person prefers taupe to purple, why someone once liked shag carpets and now giggles at them. The fickle nature of fad and fashion should make only the brave enter the consumer market. While the consumer market has great volume (which does not always translate into equivalent profit), you should enter this market only if you are introducing a new category of consumer product with a dependable and very well understood demand. Companies already in retail, by contrast, will be desperate to buy profit tools. The great consumer empires will always be fewer than those of the tool builders.

The tool builders have been with us since the dawn of humanity, and they are responsible for humanity's progress. The computer industry has prospered so mightily precisely because it is a tool builder. The original IBM mainframes and today's servers are sold to businesses, not to the retail market. Indeed, until recently most computing machinery was exactly that: machinery for business. For most of its history, even the "personal" computer was used only by knowledge workers in organizations large and small. The small business/home-office market for computing products remains important and much coveted. (Now, of course, the personal computer has become a retail product — a communications and entertainment product — whose demand is much less assured and thus much more volatile.)

Tool makers have always been society's most valued members, and so they shall be in the future. The only difference now is that the tool builders have been given their ultimate device: computing, humanity's most flexible tool. Society now merely waits for the tool makers and their customers to truly appreciate what might be done, to appreciate that an entire array of stunning tools is about to change the workplace beyond recognition. This great endeavour will leave the new century transformed. The Internet is no more than the stage upon which the drama is presented.

While there will be many kinds of computer-related profit tools, the predominant ones will be those of universal applicability — the only way *all* businesses can be helped in *all* their functions. Increasing competition is raising the standard of performance of all workers. From the shop-floor worker to the chief executive officer, there must be faster responses, fewer mistakes, and fewer resources used. Each new challenge is essentially an information problem, a decision-making problem.

The market's voice was muffled recently by the thunder of the herd, which picked up the scent of easy riches in fantasy and folklore. They repeated to each other the mantra of technology: as if by magic, all tech stocks could rise 40 percent per year forever. Neither patience nor plan, work nor insight, was allegedly necessary. But the moment passed, as all aberrations do.

Today, the market could not speak more clearly. There must be a plan and a strategy. There must be sales and profits. The forecast of business conditions must be logical and supported by evidence. It demands help to make better decisions, about innovation, markets, and costs. No matter how good the decision today, it must be made better tomorrow. These decision tools, also called expert systems, are computing's highest purpose.

CHAPTER TWO

EXPERT SYSTEMS:
THE ULTIMATE TECHNOLOGY

MASTER OR TECHNICIAN?

What is so radically different about expert systems? How can they be created and made to operate effectively? The first hurdle is technical. Creating software involves two fundamental concerns: executing an instruction in a computable form, and determining what the instruction should be. The first concern takes the instruction as given and concentrates on producing the computable solution (that is, the software program). This vast undertaking consumes most of the computing industry's resources, since the process of executing an instruction is highly complex and demands great technical skill, effort, and time. Indeed, to most observers, the software industry's *only* concern seems to be the task of executing a computable instruction set. Not surprisingly, the education of software professionals concentrates on this skill, as does academic and private-sector research. The emphasis on new software tools such as artificial intelligence (AI, which is designed to simulate human thought) is thus not surprising.

It is well understood that creating reliable code is no easy matter. The supply of those with the requisite talent is inadequate to meet the demand. And even those with talent, working within reasonable time-lines, struggle to ship bug-free software. However, the second part of the software challenge, determining what the instructions themselves should be, what the rules should be, is largely ignored by the computing industry. This part of the challenge is equivalent to specifying the basic solution to a particular problem. But many in the computing industry believe that this is not their responsibility; they feel it is either the job of the users to specify their needs or the concern of some other discipline. Thus the industry leaves largely unexplored an entire domain of applications, the next great generation of expert software.

Unfortunately, computing is trapped by its past victories. The industry is still so new that most of its accomplishments have involved the implementation of obvious and simple solutions. Not surprisingly, computing history has been characterized by a series of rapid product introductions that have enjoyed equally rapid adoptions. This is exactly what you would expect when a new technology meets a straightforward and immediately useful application. And so the industry is always looking for the Next Quick Big Thing, the next sudden surge of demand. Its stunning success has made it very sure of itself.

When those in the industry introduce products that provide obvious solutions, their competitors must be prepared to respond quickly to duplicate their efforts. This is especially so since obvious solutions are often inherently difficult to protect as intellectual property, and therefore there are no legal barriers to entry. In this situation, speed of response, market share, branding, and leveraging an installed base become the elements essential to survival. However, when computing is applied to problems with no obvious or simple solutions, such as how to choose a senior executive or how to determine a likely line of investigation for an anti-ageing drug or a corporate strategy, it is an entirely new game — one that will have profound effects on both computing and the business world. That this single truth can unleash such dramatic changes may seem surprising, but the logic is irresistible.

It is not disparaging to say that computing software usually expresses obvious solutions. Notwithstanding the difficulty of its execution, a word-processing program is an obvious function, as is a spreadsheet, an accounting package, or any software for making an object rotate in three-dimensional space, transferring numbers, or connecting John to Mary. The Internet and many of its applications are also merely combinations of obvious functions. The advantage of these programs from the software developer's point of view is that there is little doubt about what the instruction set should accomplish. It is either immediately obvious (add to account A, subtract from account B), or it may be easily specified by the user.

It is indicative of the industry's lack of interest in the specifics of the instruction, however, that even for such straightforward tasks, the client's requirements are often not fully determined. The industry is rightly famous for its disconnection from the end-user, as well as for its often thoroughly inadequate liaising, even in explicitly customized development. All too often, software is so awkward that the user is left wondering what the developer was even trying to do. The developer's common rebuttal that the problem was a technically necessary constraint is too easy an answer. Often developers misunderstand the function they are trying to execute for the simple reason that they have never performed the task themselves, nor have they seen the need to consult with those who do perform it. Developers do not always recognize that their internal environments are quite unlike those of the typical corporate knowledge worker. Without that understanding, they build software — office suites, for example — that are flexible, able to do practically everything. But because they can do everything, they do nothing especially well or easily, from word processing to database management. To overcome this difficulty, the users are supposed to reconfigure their machines to match their personal needs. But that process is itself complex and uncertain, and the act of removing the ranks of unrecognizable icons will not provide a function that is altogether absent from the program.

Many search engines, in particular, appear to have been designed by people who have never spent days searching for information — never mind made searching for information their life's work. How else can we account for the fact that search engines often lack the most logical procedures and make it nearly impossible to perform functions manually? The developer's typical answer to these complaints is to direct the user to read the manual. In other words, it is the user's fault. And when it is observed that most workers do not have the time to read these complex manuals, the developer's shrugged response is that they must find the time. But millions of dissatisfied users cannot be dismissed as just unreasonably demanding consumers. It should give everyone pause to recall that this assignment of blame to the consumer is the oldest marketing mistake in commercial history.

When a problem does not have an obviously simple or known solution, an instruction set, of course, cannot be specified either easily or sometimes at all. The superficial reaction of computing experts to this self-evident observation, to the extent that they think about it at all, is to wait for users to take action and specify the solution (that is, the rules), if they so choose. It may seem logical to suggest that software developers cannot create a program to solve a problem that no one else knows how to solve (or solve easily). But this is a thoroughly inappropriate response; users will not be able to solve many of these problems if they act without the involvement of computing specialists. The computing industry fails to see this dilemma principally because too many of its members see themselves as pure technicians executing someone else's orders. Whether those orders are simple ones delivered through the marketplace or more complex ones provided by a client is irrelevant; the choice is to react or to create.

Of course, there are many companies and industrial sectors that are largely reactive, although business schools almost with one voice decry such lack of initiative. Still, these reactors can often eke out a reasonable profit. Unfortunately, those in the software industry will find it extremely difficult to retreat to the ranks of plausibly profitable yet plodding companies. The software industry's entire economic logic and financial resources are based on the fact that many of its founders, executives, employees, and investors lust for commercial empire and its scale of wealth. Indeed, it is the lure of profit that fuels the industry's extraordinary growth. But if software continues to insist on executing only the rules it is given, it imperils these ambitions. Although the superb technicians at Microsoft and Oracle built empires, they managed to do so because they took the rules as simple and nearly self-evident. But the easy rules have been used up (with the exception of the interactive toaster), and even the first empires are struggling to maintain their position. Those who follow in the technicians' reactive mode will fare even worse.

However, there is an alternative view of computing, and those exploring the marketplace will find it in due course. Whether software developers or others will fully realize this opportunity is the only point of debate. And when that opportunity becomes engaged, computing will evolve into humanity's principal information tool, in fact instead of in rhetoric.

This alternative view is centred on a fundamental understanding of the role of information in society. Any problem sits somewhere on a continuum that runs from simple to complex. Computing helps solve problems by searching for and interpreting information, also on a scale ranging from simple to complex. The output produced for the user ranges from raw data to partial solutions to complete solutions. This output is delivered in a form that ranges from message to decision. Expert systems represent the complex end of all three of these scales. They conduct complex search and interpretive procedures to produce partial to complete solutions that appear as advice, recommendations, or decisions. Advice, recommendation, and decisions are distinguished the degree to which further human response is required before action can ensue. Advice is simply helpful guidance offered to a decision-maker. Recommendations comprise detailed advice but fall short of a complete answer. A decision is a plan of action that is ready to be implemented,

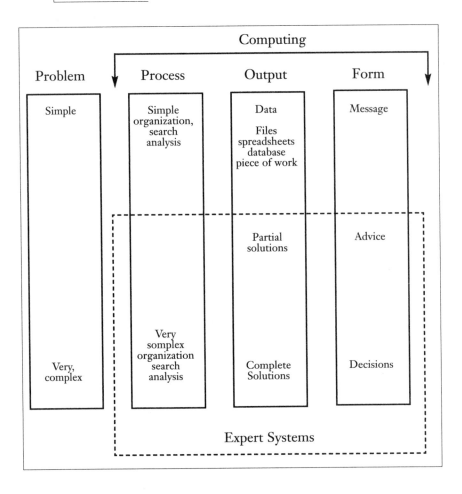

and often this plan requires only approval or (depending on the circumstances) continuing oversight. This framework is presented in the diagram above, and the scope of expert systems is indicated.

For simpler problems, there is an array of existing computing tools, from search engines to spreadsheets, with more on the way. Complex problems, by contrast, usually need the rule-intensity of an expert system, and the number of such systems is growing slowly compared to the market need. For routine problems (e.g., what is the temperature in Cairo, what is the price-earnings ratio of Cisco Systems, who is the vice-president of Chase Manhattan, what is the atomic weight of oxygen, what is the *Wall Street Journal* saying about Lucent Technologies, what is the consumer price index for the past month), computing needs to use relatively straightforward search tools and almost no analysis; it produces data in a message that is simply communicated to the user. Of course, this information can be very useful, even valuable, and executing the software to perform this function is often difficult. But the relative complexity of the process of creating the software is a separate issue. It is excluded from the diagram so we can maintain our focus on what software can and should do, not on how the software should or could be created.

The next range of somewhat more complex problems involves issues such as how to file, organize, sort, and manipulate text and images. Instead of posing the simple queries described above, the user is now asking the computer to help create work, whether that work is a memorandum, an address directory, or a financial statement. Output is delivered as files, spreadsheets, and databases, though these all still largely appear as messages on the user's screen (or on multiple users' screens). This area has been reasonably well developed as the computing industry works its way up the scale of difficulty.

Then there are the problems that require considerable mathematical calculation and deliver output as a finished, stand-alone piece of work; the types of software that address these problems include most programs for graphic design and computer-assisted design (CAD), as well as all manner of financial performance tools. A digital dinosaur or an electronic circuit represents the resulting pieces of work.

This particular range of computing solutions only approaches the characteristics of the expert system. But in spite of its elaborate array of mathematical rules, this type of programming does not produce advice. (The CAD program becomes a complete expert only when it advises on good design or commercially attractive design.) The continuing development of this category of software is driven either by the need to advance the mathematical techniques that deliver the function or by a desire to determine how the mathematical rules can be made computable.

Expert systems appear as a program begins to provide advice or make decisions regarding complex problems (that is, ones that often require continuing sensitivity to the external environment in the presence of many variables). Present applications are largely in the field of process control; this includes systems that monitor and control everything from petrochemical plants to electrical utilities to the great communications networks. Computer-assisted manufacturing (CAM) systems build cars and process food. Other expert systems address inventory flow and the broader issues of demand and supply-chain management. They also address enterprise-resource planning, customer-relationship management, financial- and commodities-market trading. The output of these systems facilitates business activity and, in some cases, is integrated into the overall business operation. The above areas of activity include expert systems of various degrees of rule-intensity; some need more rules or more interrelated rules than others.

Like all expert systems, these applications search, find, and/or monitor data that they then subject to rule-bound analysis. Depending on the rule complexity, some of these programs can be at the boundary between expert systems and good software. And there is little doubt that some of the systems could benefit from having either more rules or better rules, or both.

The last band of expert systems tackles the most complex business, scientific, and human problems. Business problems include such questions as how executives should be chosen and compensated, how a company can find competitive advantage, what might be a better marketing strategy, where tomorrow's dangers lie, what the momentum of a particular technology is, and how R&D resources should be allocated among computing opportunities. Scientific problems include such issues as how a drug can be created, how healing after surgery can be accelerated, how a computer can operate faster, how a building can rise taller. Human problems of the appropriate scale include such questions as how to help a child to learn, how to encourage safe sex, how to create a successful song or movie. Expert systems that address human problems are particularly complex because they must take into account the constraints of physical science, human behaviour, and the dynamics of society and its marketplaces. (Curing cancer is as much about the level of funding and the behaviour of both the researcher and the patient as it is about hard science.)

THE FOREST OR THE TREES?

The task of creating expert systems is made more challenging by the fact that those who truly understand the computing function are not the same people who know (or should know) how to look for new rules systematically. This is a gulf over which little conversation passes. One side does almost no systematic search for rules, and the other does not do all that much more. Developers act only when the rules are self-evident — that is, when they require only a few easy steps, or when the developer can wait for client instructions. Textbooks on expert systems themselves pay scant attention to the procedures to be used to find solutions (that is, to find out what rules should be implemented). Their advice is often to "talk to the experts." They tend to caution that if the question being asked is not narrow and precise, the experts may "disagree." With such advice, it is all too easy to see why many expert systems remain primitive and underexploited. (A developer who merely summarizes expert opinions should write a book instead of a program.)

Moreover, users and clients do not themselves usually look for solutions systematically. They search for specific answers instead of broadly applicable ones, for immediate action instead of long-term policy. They rely on old approaches because society and its business community are conservative at heart. And of course, they do not understand well enough either information theory or computing (or their interrelationships). Given this, it is not surprising that the user does not often understand how computing applies to a task or marshals information to further the accomplishment of that task.

Surely it is not radical to suggest that computing sits at the centre of the process by which solutions are found and rules written. Better ways to collect, verify, organize, compare, and analyze information must therefore logically contribute to an improved way to identify solutions. It is logical to assume that the organization that uses computing to find or determine the rules is the one that will be able to turn the rules into software and profit from this software. That is quite apart from turning some of the search procedures into elite expert systems themselves.

But this possibility appears to interest the business world as little as it does the computing world. Indeed, who even teaches such an approach? Where are the MBA courses on information theory and computing methods? Where are the books on corporate strategy built around the computer's ability to find vacant space in the marketplace? Where are the knowledge-management manuals that deal with specifics instead of generalities? The act of trolling the Internet is in no way a coherent search, never mind a form of research. Truth does not lie in routine key-words. That anyone should think it does reveals the great competitive advantage that awaits.

Software developers, or at least the best of them, certainly are well on the way to understanding how to use computing to find or create expert rules. Moreover, computing professionals are perfectly capable of integrating information theory with computing, should they choose to do so. The point is not that software developers cannot be more than technicians, but rather that too many of them do not *want* to be more.

The most common approach used by those developers who *do* recognize the potential of expert systems is to disaggregate a problem into simple pieces that can be addressed by either straightforward computing or a system of self-evident rules. The only difference between the developer and the client in this process is that the developer can break a problem into its constituent parts with a greater degree of computer sophistication than can a client. But disaggregation works only on some problems; most truly complex problems are complex because they cannot easily be taken apart without violating their basic logic. For example, at a fundamental level, the physical interactions that produce a healthy body are based on interrelationships seen together, not alone, and certainly not in small parts. A strong circulatory system, in other words, is a function of nutrition, exercise, genetic inheritance, and an active lifestyle.

No strategic business issue is easily turned into small, self-contained bits. If a company has identified a high-priority new market, it must consider whether it has the knowledge and the people needed to create a particular product for this market. But that query naturally leads to questions about whether it will have to hire new personnel and/or buy expertise. That then leads to a consideration of whether it needs to raise more capital. But the company may be able to raise more capital because it is entering a new market. And thus the company is back where it started, each step contingent on the others. Based on the evidence, this approach works only fitfully. Nortel, by its own admission, was taken completely by surprise when the demand for its equipment plunged because, as it said, it was talking to its customers' engineers and not their treasurers. So much for strategy in bits and pieces.

We must ask ourselves whether this long-established approach of disaggregation is a feasible way to solve complex problems. Or has computing changed this situation? Does computing provide us with a new way to search for information or with a new way to search for answers? Is computing making possible a more effective search for the answers to complex problems? Will it be a process that is much, much more than just computerizing the processes of the past?

Unfortunately, both developers and custom-software designers are usually so preoccupied with executing their clients' or their industry's obvious needs that they themselves conduct little information research and fail to see the benefit of doing more. A further discouragement to conducting this research is the difficulty that developers encounter when trying to understand a user's problem in cases where the user does not know what the solution is. Of course, the user is also often at a loss to understand how a piece of information not yet known or a piece of software not yet created might address the problem. The answer is, of course, an intimately collaborative approach to research for software development. This collaboration could be initiated by either the user or the developer.

However, when the process is initiated by users, it will be focused on their particular goals and the developer will be little more than a custom designer. When the process is initiated by the software developer, the broader potential of the approach, as a computer tool, can be maximized. Currently, most players are waiting for a response from the other side, and as a result, business problems remain unsolved and software remains undeveloped. The rare collaborations achieve both impressive results and a competitive advantage over less alert colleagues. For example, BlueNexus, a company specializing in logistics software, has enjoyed rapid success throughout North America. Its product, which schedules the routes of commercial vehicles and manages employee workload, meets the exact needs of the marketplace because it was created in close association with a key logistic operator who is now a partner in BlueNexus.

While both user and developer often fail to recognize the scale of the collaborative opportunity, the developer should see the matter more clearly. For one thing, the developer, as an outsider, can bring a creative objectivity to the problem that a user's organizational dynamics may impede. But most essentially, there are usually information-related problems — too much or too little information; information too poorly organized or too poorly distributed. More often than not, the solution is the creation of new software tools, not the more effective use of existing tools. But the scale of the research needed to create tools for problems with complex solutions will often be so great that its cost would have to be distributed over many users.

The large and powerful consulting industries have a logical role to play in the development of expert systems. After all, they sell expertise and offer solutions to complex problems. Moreover, many consultants specialize explicitly in information management or computing (which should not be, but often are, different specialties), and help their clients implement improved information-management tools and techniques. Whether these consultants concentrate on narrow technical issues or broad strategic ones, they can provide value and contribute to the process of getting problems solved.

However, relatively few consultants, of whatever specialty, see themselves as developers of expert systems, and their own view of strategic information is often constrained. Consultants are also trying to satisfy the client's objectives, which can be especially difficult when the client has no particular understanding of what to ask for. The consultants' typical response is not to research a generalized answer, but to use their existing expertise to offer a specific answer to the client's most immediate need. Of course, the consultants may also realize that if they provide a general answer instead of a specific one, their clients will not actually need to use their services so often. That alarming thought hardly warms them to the idea of the widespread use of expert systems in any of their various guises.

Also, to search for answers systematically, to experiment with new approaches (and break established practice), to produce a generalized protocol for a set of problems — all these require a considerable amount of speculative work. Such research involves much effort and expense, and because it is an exploration of the unknown, a successful outcome cannot be guaranteed. Hence, the risk discourages research, especially for those consultants who would have to fund it from their cash flow of billable hours. However, as we will see in chapter 11, consultants, although somewhat slow to join the "expert system party," are destined to lead the marketing charge.

TRUE DAWN

There are those who believe that computing will have a great social effect even without expert systems. These people speak of the Web and the great digital community that is being created. They speak of a Web that will meld together great tagged databases that will be easy to search and offer deep insight. That this will happen in due course is likely. But it fails to speak to the real problem. It simply assumes that more information is better than less information, that more accessible information is better than less accessible information, and that the more you pump up the accessibility of humanity's knowledge, the more answers to complex solutions will simply appear. But these databases will fail to realize their potential without calling on powerful expert systems to enter and create solutions. The Web is always a facilitator, never a creator. Without expert systems, you could not navigate this vast base of interconnected data. You could not organize it or make sense of it, and you certainly could not massage it into rules (that is, actionable solutions). Not only does dependence on Web-linked data raise the volume problem to an ever greater degree, it also ignores several serious issues.

It ignores the fact that much of the information that is in the databases today is incomplete, out of context, uninterpretable, and/or wrong. The hotel reservation system, for example, may assume you are a smoker even though you requested a non-smoking room the last time you booked. The department store database has your purchases filed so many different ways it cannot create an overall profile of you or your needs. The personnel records from five years ago are inaccessible because the computer system was upgraded. The inventory statistics are three months out of date. And the sales figures for the past quarter that are being down-loaded by the enterprise-planning software are simply wrong.

Without expert systems to improve the quality of the information, interconnecting databases is simply a convenient way to spread error. And there is no reason to assume that these databases will necessarily be used — or used aggressively. It is not at all clear that people who do not use physical libraries today would in any organized way use digital libraries. And there is no particular reason why they would use digital libraries that are so huge as to be even more intimidating than the virtual libraries that already exist. The assumption that people love to read, to do research, to pursue the truth — in short, that people love learning — is simplistic and all too naive.

The expert system, by contrast, knows no such human frailties. It advances into the jungle of information without fear, favour, or fatigue. It has its orders; it marches on.

But how do we actually make it work?

Consider a company that operates a theme park simulating the planet Mars, both its reality and its place in science-fiction literature. The park's managers wish to use an expert system for day-to-day operations. It occurs to them that if such a system is successful, they can expand the approach to other areas of the business. Having found no off-the-shelf system that can be customized to address the particular aspects of the park's management, however, they decide to create their own system. After all, this will give them a tool not available to their competitors.

The managers' first step is to acquire the IT talent they need for such an aggressive system. Ideally, they want to find a software company that has experience in expert systems related to park management, and that is interested in acquiring a new client or partner. Negotiations, perhaps heated, will lead to an agreement about costs, the division of rewards, and intellectual property. The park's only other options are to expand its own IT department and/or to use contract consultants.

Next comes the research. The software company and its developers must learn both park management in general and the particular demands of their unique property. The first step is to debrief all current park employees and all former management employees. What worked in the past? What failed? Why? This process is often lengthy, as it can be difficult to obtain and record the observations.

In the beginning, the observations go into nothing more than a flexible, easily searched database. And already senior managers use their judgement to suggest priorities for the information. The CEO, for example, emphasizes that he thinks the variability of the weather is the biggest operational problem, while someone else thinks it is the perishable nature of the food service's inventory. But these suggestions of priority are only noted, not assigned. It is far too early to decide anything.

The company would then draw on every other available source of park management information, digital and otherwise. This process can be made more efficient with expert information systems, but in the end, real people will do much reading. At this stage, some common themes or packages of advice are becoming apparent. But it is still too early to decide on any of the rules for sure.

Using the most advanced search tools, the company and its developers look for any challenges to the information already compiled. If one source argued for the park's maintenance function to be contracted out, they will look for one that argued the reverse. And who decides which argument is correct? If no data tip the balance, the CEO decides. That is what defines leadership in the information age.

Since it will also be clear that part of the park's management challenge is to accommodate a wide range of influences, from the weather and school holidays to delivery delays, some time must be spent finding the best source of information for each of these concerns. The park will have dozens of such external information links.

Finally, employees will comb through all of the company's internal records, looking for any kind of systematic relationships between the demand for the park's services and the resources used to satisfy them.

With all the information assembled and recorded in a searchable format, the specification of rules begins. Logically enough, the process begins with the company's existing rules, vague and inconsistent though they may be. The company will organize any existing rules into such categories as customer safety, maintenance, food service, ticketing, crowd control, and so on. Now the managers stop reading and start talking a lot. The developers shift from speculators to active participants as they insist on clear, computable rules using today's software technology.

Dozens or even hundreds of proposed rules will be generated. Some will clash with others, as discussion will make clear. Others will be shown to be redundant or even wrong on further examination. In due course, the process gathers momentum and rules are more easily generated. If there are more than one hundred visitors on the simulated landing zone, send entertainers at once to the entry point to slow down the influx of traffic. If the weather is going to be perfect *and* there is a school holiday, order twice as many hot dogs and half as much chicken because the visitor mix will skew towards children. If the weather is expected to be hot and humid, double the number of staff at the first aid station. Based on past evidence, as expressed in the attendance rules, tomorrow's visitor count will be between 3,000 and 4,000. And so on.

Rules will also have to be assigned priority. While this prioritization will ultimately be done by discussion and executive decision, the expert system can be run in trial under different scenario loadings. This allows the park's operations to be simulated, which will reveal that, for example, under some circumstances, the rules have everyone in the park dead from starvation. Better to meet this in simulation, where a reprogrammed line of code can correct the result.

There is, of course, one kind of priority that expert systems need not establish. Both computers and humans must order tasks when one is logically dependent on another for completion (for example, the estimated number of visitors must precede the determination of the next day's staffing levels). But while the human decision-makers must make some of their already limited time available for the ordering of tasks, the expert system knows no such need. Thus while the manager's highest daily priority may be to maintain control of the cash flow, and only then to deal with absent employees and a missed delivery date, the expert system can respond and issue instructions simultaneously. This attribute alone accounts for much of the expert system's advantage. It never sleeps, and it parallel-processes.

Yet notwithstanding all this research and analysis, there is no reason to believe that the company will produce, at once or ever, the perfect park management system. There will, without doubt, be failures, *as there are without expert systems.* But the effect of these failures is very different when an expert system is not in place. When human managers fail, the most common response is to fix the problem, avoid blame, and move on. And even when at least some attempt is made to understand why the failure occurred, the answer often provokes no systematic response and is later forgotten. By contrast, the expert system's very structure demands a careful re-examination and a coded solution. With humans, given their vague unpredictability, there is always the hope that they will stumble onto a better response; with expert systems, they *must* find a better answer to avoid repeating the mistakes of the past.

As the park develops its expert system, it is in effect creating a continuously evolving experiment in how to best manage its facility. The system documents what it knows and makes sure it finds out what it needs to know. Knowledge is guarded, not forgotten; used, not disregarded. There is logic and the test of observed results. Expert systems are human activities conducted according to the scientific method.

THE WAY AHEAD

With competition insistently demanding improved innovation, efficiency, and marketing, expert systems are the only technology that can come to the rescue. Because expert systems operate at the decision-gate, the starting point for all action, they are the only technology that can truly strengthen any aspect of business. No other technology can make that claim credibly. While the Internet does indeed *touch* almost every decision being made, it does not actually improve the decision-making process. Two misinformed people talking to each other do not automatically see the light.

Moreover, only expert systems offer the continuing possibility of better decisions and therefore more effective business responses. As humanity learns, so do the expert systems. So long as humanity can learn, the expert systems will advance. In this new universe, the octopus-like communication pipes of the Internet serve a far humbler purpose. What matters is the content of information flowing on the Internet and the means to interpret that content. Without expert systems, the interpretation and mobilization of expertise are impossible. In due course, expert systems will guide us in all we do — teaching, reminding, warning, and on occasion, stopping us.

CHAPTER THREE

THE POWER
OF THE RULE

HOT AIR

Even though force of habit, limited perspective, and lack of imagination have slowed the creation of expert systems, they will nevertheless inevitably grow into the largest category of software, far exceeding the sales of Internet applications. There can be no doubt that the market for "work" tools is greater than the market for "talk" tools. The value of work is still (thankfully) many times the value of communication. Equally important is the fact that expert systems as work tools earn their own keep — that is, they *directly* generate value by lowering costs, increasing sales, or improving products. The developer can ask for a premium price for his expert system because there is a direct connection between it and the value it creates. Improved decision making about cost is clearly tied to profitability, and nothing else need be said.

Ordinary software has no such automatic value link. Operating systems are necessary for computing, and computing contributes to value. But the connection is much less direct — and sometimes not apparent at all. It is, for example, not clear how Windows NT makes a business more money. There is an argument that it does, but it is a less immediate and often contentious argument. Equally indirect is the argument for everything from spreadsheets to word processing to databases.

The connection between enhanced communication and profitability is even more indirect. Of course, without communication, modern commerce is impossible; indeed, commercial transactions themselves become impossible. But the correlation between more talk and more profit is much less clear, if only because of all the intervening steps that must occur before the one actually creates the other. There is no question why it is difficult to make money from the Internet itself: it cannot charge its customers for the service of communication because they are *already* connected. It must therefore sell them even *more* communication services. So, of course, it must be priced at the margin. Unless e-mail really is inexpensive, customers will use the alternative. The alternatives, then, like voice transmission, also have no choice but to join the fray by bidding down the price. Talk is after all cheap, in more ways than one. Action — that is, work — is what society and the marketplace really value. This profound distinction between expert systems and communication facilitation is at the heart of the way ahead.

The market demand for expert systems is much greater than the supply now available, and very much greater than is commonly recognized. And what the market wants, the market gets. The only question is how quickly. To those who want to create, use, or invest in expert systems, there is a window of great competitive advantage. From the business user's point of view, the obstacle is the lack of understanding of how expert systems can increase profits, how they work. (The obstacle from the developer's perspective was discussed in the previous chapter.)

CHICKEN BONES?

There should be little mystery about how and why expert systems work. First, rules work, as any cook, engineer, or scientist knows. To reject rules is to reject technology and the scientific method. But it is not a criticism to say that the rules do not *always* work. They certainly do not. When they do not work, however, there are only three non-superstitious reasons why: the rule itself was wrong; the rule was improperly applied; or there is no rule for that problem . . . yet. The logic of the rule still stands, however. It is the role of expert systems to make sure rules are followed properly, and to encourage the development of more and better rules.

Nevertheless, there are many people who do not believe in rules *in general*. They understand and accept that rules sometimes apply, as, for example, in a piece of machinery or in a trajectory to the moon. More or less, they accept the rules (that is, the laws) of physics, while claiming to keep an open mind about the presence of aliens among us or the dangers of smoking. But when it comes to the rest of the human experience, beyond the confines of some aspects of the physical sciences, they accept the applicability of the rules much less readily. The market seems to many business executives to be beyond rules, or at least beyond the known rules. To work in the marketplace, they believe, is a voyage of discovery, both experiential and intuitive. "Run it up the flagpole to see who salutes." "Let's roll the dice." "Let's see what happens." These approaches act as an excuse for a lack of thought, and they are an invitation to agile improvisation. This is the antithesis of reasoned decision making. This is a strategy built on making mistakes until (if you survive) you finally get it right. The waste of resources is beyond calculation.

Of course, there are uncertainties in the marketplace that are beyond any known rule (as there are in physics). But the presence of a *degree* of uncertainty does not justify the abandonment or, more typically, erratic use of the rules of the marketplace. There is not much uncertainty about the first rule of business: no profit, no enterprise.

WATCH THE CLOCK!

Expert systems produce better decisions, decisions that increase profit in several ways. First, they save time. The expert systems deliver answers in the form of either advice or action. They will advise the user when the senior marketing manager's performance is deficient (and will suggest the company either train or fire the person). They will suggest a complex series of steps to hedge against the uncertainty of oil prices. Or they will directly order the factory in Trenton, New Jersey, to make and ship product to Sears' distribution warehouse in New York. They do not deliver more than is needed to read, digest, or consider. They therefore speed the decision-making process: more decisions can be made more quickly. This is an essential function, since expert systems are responding to competitive conditions that demand ever faster responses. Time is not only money, it is a rapidly appreciating currency.

The Internet, by contrast, is a sinkhole of time. How could it not be? It's a bottomless pit of the good, the bad, and the ugly, littered with an infinite set of rubbish and riches. It overwhelms the decision-maker as often as it enlightens; by delivering too much information of uncertain value, the Internet inevitably slows the decision-maker.

Some would be tempted to argue that the Internet has already increased the speed of decision making in some areas, such as, for example, distribution (demand/supply chain) management. However, it is in fact the expert rules that deliver superior distribution management (i.e., that send goods). The act of interconnection does not actually produce the essential effect of smoothly adjusting distribution chains. We must stop referring to any innovation that accesses the communication network as Internet technology. Customer-relationship software is an expert system that runs very well on the Internet but would (and does) also work on the ancient analogue telephone system. Even business auction sites are a function of their software, and thus could feasibly be run over the telephone network. To think of these examples as "Internet effects" is to distract the user and the developer from establishing better rules and making better use of the "rule tools." (Again, we reiterate that we are not making light of the powerful effect of cheap communications; we merely ask that it be recognized for what it is, and that we be allowed to move on to more complex matters.)

The second reason why expert systems produce profitable decisions is that their answers are more likely to be correct. Examples already abound. Financial institutions now make faster and more accurate decisions about the creditworthiness of customers by using expert risk-assessment tools. That means a credit card limit can be raised within minutes and a mortgage approved in a day. In a different area of business, Wal-Mart's inventory-control system makes sure that merchandise is where customers want it when they want it. It prevents unsold goods from sitting lost in the warehouse. Eaton's, by contrast, often did not know how much inventory it had, never mind where.

Correct decisions save the time and resources wasted by incorrect decisions, identify opportunities before the competition does, and direct resources to the best (that is, the highest return) use. By minimizing incorrect decisions, expert systems speed corporate responses and sharpen every aspect of corporate performance. We note these obvious effects since in spite of the fact that they are readily apparent, companies rarely spend much time and effort on developing any systematic program to improve the quality of their decision making (other than training employees or flooding managers with more information they cannot read).

While training is a worthy and useful function, it is also expensive and of varying quality (like much education). Moreover, in a rapidly changing environment, training can easily lag behind the immediate need. Also, training is usually directed at helping an employee or a manager deal with a specific new task or problem. It rarely deals with the underlying causes of incorrect decisions — like gullibility, for example, or a lack of appreciation for the need to use factual evidence to make business decisions. These issues, of course, were supposed to have been addressed by the manager's general education.

However, no matter how well or how aggressively training is undertaken, it still does not address the single greatest barrier to accurate decision making: the lack of time. In the face of mounting competitive pressures, there is less and less time to think about pending decisions. There is less time to consider, to challenge, to gather and evaluate evidence, even to read. There is less time to take advantage of one's training, education, or experience. And while no alert manager could fail to see time as the great enemy, corporations still reduce their ranks arbitrarily — without reducing the amount of work to be done. Thus the time pressure on the typical manager grows even fiercer. The result is that the downsized company gets a short-term bump-up in its earnings, while the quality of its decision making degrades over the longer term. It is not surprising that many of these downsized companies lurch to and fro as they struggle forward.

Yet even without the downsizing effect, competition tightens time constraints and causes the quality of decision making to deteriorate. But with each problem created, the market also offers an opportunity. The solution is present in the expert system that invites the manager to let *someone else* decide (or at least take over part of the decision-making burden). The expert system is the decision-maker that never sleeps. Either we accept its help or we will watch our decision making become progressively more inept, eventually buckling under the pressure of time itself.

The time constraint alone justifies expert systems as an indispensable and high-priority business tool. Moreover, it is a tool that can be tailored to a particular situation. It can be everything from an adviser on call, waiting to be queried by the manager, to an active participant, running continuously and reserving the right to interject a recommendation or a warning at any time. In certain critical applications, the expert system may prevent the manager from making an "incorrect" decision. Of course, in other situations, the expert system will itself implement a decision with no human notice or intervention (as occurs in industrial and inventory-control processes).

As accelerating competition and technological change force increasingly rapid decision making and punish incorrect decisions ever more harshly, expert systems will both *save* time and *take* time. They save the decision-maker's time while they, the expert systems, take *their* time to deliver decisions that are more accurate. In essence, expert systems offer a critically important time bonus to the entire business world, its participants, and its processes.

THE PHILOSOPHER'S STONE

There is no doubt about what the expert system will take its time to do. Nor is there any doubt that these functions will improve the quality of decision making. Expert systems do no more than what the basic philosophical principles of decision making require. They will first make sure that no logical or empirical relationship, no rule, is forgotten or omitted. In other words, the expert system will plug the gaps in the decision-making process, making sure that no key step is disregarded because the decision-maker forgot it, never learned it, or was never even exposed to it in the first place.

Consider the expert systems that assess the risk of a loan or an investment. They exist and are being further developed. Such a risk-assessment system can serve either as an adviser or as an absolute decision-gate, depending on the expression of corporate policy. First, it will establish a series of steps through which any loan or investment must proceed. In other words, the decision-making framework is established and enforced. This structure becomes the corporation's specifically defined approach to risk-taking. No longer can a manager forget step 3 or substitute an approach of his or her own.

Each step has precisely defined rules to determine whether the investment should or should not move forward. For example, the expert system will require the ratio of collateral value to liabilities to fall within prescribed norms. As well, the conflicts and tradeoffs between the rules have *already* been specified. Loans will not be granted arbitrarily and inconsistently, depending on the mood of the lending officer.

Having secured the decision-making framework, the expert system mobilizes all the available information that is applicable to the decision at hand. While this process guards against the inadvertent omission of data from the pool of readily available information, it also searches for additional information more aggressively and completely than any human agent has the time to do. The risk-assessment tool, for example, will draw on a much greater range of information than was previously feasible. The expert system can absorb the loan applicant's entire marketing plan and subject it to analysis. It can include variables on the macroeconomic environment and the relevant industry trends. Indeed, expert systems have had such a significant impact in the financial sector because only they can analyze the vast amounts of information currently available for such products as derivative investments.

Expert systems in their most highly developed states also screen the entire decision flow to remove mistakes, especially errors of fact or logic. This function addresses the ancient GIGO (garbage in/garbage out) computing rule by doing something about it (instead of merely reciting it). This issue is discussed in more detail below.

Last and not least, the expert system will search for better rules — cause-and-effect relationships. At one level, this requires the system to do no more than search all the scholarly and business literature to look for a new idea that can be applied to the problem at hand. It can collect all the commentary by any individual whose past contributions to risk analysis are well known. Of course, the expert system could not automatically input the new rules. It would, however, draw them to the attention of its creators. In the context of credit assessment, this could be a new piece of published research that reveals a correlation between new product introductions and corporate success. These above procedures are already being used, although far less aggressively than they should be. The fact that the expert system will not always find better rules does not detract from what the search itself will add to the decision-making process.

While there is no doubt that the above functions will add to the quality of any decision, there is equally no doubt that they can be performed by an expert system. There is nothing impossible about creating a rule that says you must use all the rules that you or the world already has on any particular subject. At its most elemental level, this is no more than a checklist. Search engines exist to find and assemble information, and they can be used both more aggressively and more creatively than most people have the time for. There is nothing impossible about checking a fact with its source to avoid acting on mistaken information, to confirm that the data is current, or to ensure that a rule has been successfully tested. And there is no reason why search tools cannot look for better rules, the latest rule, or the rule with the most evidence backing it up.

Each of these functions takes us back into the heart of computing. Since expert systems work to improve the quality of decision making of all kinds, they are essentially about information. Or more properly speaking, they are about the rules that govern the use of information to make decisions. Questions about how to manage, organize, extract, and validate information are critical for both computing and the business world. Discovering how to call forth meaning from information is an even more important problem. Information, computing, and expert systems all meet on common ground. Their interrelationships will be the defining characteristic of the new century, affecting every institution of society.

Nevertheless, it may seem that this description of expert systems is unrealistically positive. And the limitations need to be clearly noted: expert systems will make mistakes, and they will not apply easily (if at all) to those situations requiring true creativity. Instead, the argument is merely that they will function better than humans in many of our present kinds of work. They already work so well, in fact, that they are indispensable for inventory control and much of manufacturing and finance. They are present elsewhere too, in such fields as marketing and communications, and their use there also grows. It seems reasonable to assume that all repetitious work is similar enough that what works for finance will work in many other areas.

Of course, the GIGO rule will still apply to some degree. We do not now, nor will we soon, live in a thoroughly enlightened world. Thus flawed rules will be used by some systems, and incorrect tradeoffs among the rules will be made by others. However, once a rule is revealed to be flawed, the structured approach of the expert system requires it to be expunged. A bogus correlation between collateral and creditworthiness, for example, can just be deleted. As well, the expert system, as we shall see below, emphatically holds the human decision-maker and the system creator to account.

But the key point is that with the expert system, the likelihood of error will fall because there will have been at least an attempt to use humanity's accumulated knowledge. We live in so imperfect a world that the attempt alone is an uncommon event, and surely we will wish to encourage or insist on it.

The key to understanding the potential of expert systems lies in recognizing why it is so difficult to find the information and the rules necessary to make effective decisions. Why does it take so long to find what we need, so long to detect errors and omissions? The answer could hardly be plainer: we live in information chaos, compounded by information overload, with the Internet both servant and scourge.

KEEP IT SIMPLE, STUPID

The "keep it simple, stupid" (KISS) rule can be considered the expert developers' unofficial slogan. Their goal is to make sure that the end-users do not decide anything unless they have to. Since there is too much to know, too much to learn, the developers make the machine do the work whenever possible. This is clearly what most software does *not* do. It first makes the user learn all manner of new things about itself (that is, of course, not a good start to saving time), then it asks a seemingly endless series of questions. It asks to be reconfigured and then reconfigured again; boxes pop up all over the place demanding notice or attention. Spreadsheets expect a user to know how to use them as a piece of software *and* as an analytical tool, even though the first-time user does not understand the former and may not know how to do the latter. From word processing to databases to graphic-design tools, the user is supposed to "learn the software" and otherwise know about language style, library science, and the principles of design. Expert systems bury all that clutter and ask the user only for a task. As much as possible, the software does the rest. The most logical application of expert rules is, of course, to software itself.

Computers should first use expert rules on themselves. Let the software run itself, applying the rules for its own operation (why does the user have to do all that clicking?). And then the expert system can apply the rules with respect to the function being undertaken. So, for example, statistical programs will provide both the output and the rules for its interpretation.

The objections will come quickly. Adding so many rules, it is claimed, will make the program "run slow." But the user wants the program to run fast only because he has too much to do to wait for the program to go to its next step. The environment within which the expert system operates is entirely different. While the expert system will run more slowly, the user is off doing other work, not sitting at the screen, waiting. The user may actually be thinking, plotting, planning, or scheming.

Another objection is that this array of complex rules will overpower the ordinary PC. This is a truly strange argument, since it suggests that the reason software is poor is because personal computers are inadequate tools to produce useful work. This is not what one would have thought the PC manufacturers would wish to claim. Indeed, one would have thought the tool was matched to the work, and not the other way around. Perhaps the argument is actually that the developers will only make stuff that can be readily sold to the enormous installed base of existing PCs.

But while the constraints of the PC may discourage developers of expert systems, the need for power brings joy to the heart of every hardware manufacturer. As Intel and its competitors create ever more powerful microprocessors, they must worry about the purposes to which these chips will be applied. It is not all that surprising that the low end of the PC market seems not to want better chips, or that the rest of the PC market seems uncertain or actually "mature." The real difficulty may be that the hardware manufacturers are already offering tools that outstrip the imagination of developers. But expert systems will inevitably ask for more speed and power. They will demand the upgrading of computer hardware significantly and over time. That fact, as much as anything else, will cause the hardware manufacturers to become some of the most vociferous advocates of expert systems.

ONE SIZE FITS ALL

Finally, it is argued that if software was to become more rule-intensive (and thus easier to use), it would become impractical, both technically and economically, even with reasonable increases in PC capabilities. A vast number of rules would be necessary, it is claimed, because business software can be used for so many different purposes. Of course, it can, and that is exactly the compelling point. Again, the software industry tends to see every issue only one way — yesterday's way. It is not likely that a particular expert system will work for every person on earth; it won't even work for every knowledge worker, every businessperson, or even every executive in a single industry. Of course, a lot of contemporary software works only adequately. Many existing tools take a horrendous amount of time to learn because they are not actually designed *specifically* for the user. The software industry quite naturally seeks maximum sales with minimum development cost. This has led to the creation of platform products that are generically universal tools that everyone can use . . . barely. It is difficult to use most of the software because so much of it is not designed for the specific user. Therefore, users must in fact turn themselves into something they are not. They must reorganize their own work. They must push, shove, poke, and prod before they can make most pieces of software work for them.

The software industry counters with a complex discussion about how expensive it is to do development. Unless costs can be spread over many, many users, the argument goes, software would be prohibitively expensive. But the argument is all too often circular. Software does not work very well because it is generic, and because it does not work very well, the consumer does not want to pay a premium price for it. Developers, seeing that consumers do not want to pay a premium price, redouble their efforts to create products of universal applicability. Moreover, say the developers, if they can still make vast profits by proceeding in this way, why would they stop?

Putting aside the fact that many developers are not particularly profitable (exceptions such as Microsoft notwithstanding), there should be a turn towards specificity because almost all the simple applications for which generic solutions *might* be appropriate already exist. The question is what to do next. Yet the old model of do it one way and sell it to a billion people continues to be the holy grail of the computing industry. While that tendency was always acute enough, the Internet makes it an even more self-destructive avenue. Now no developer can avoid thinking about how cool it would be to sell one thing to each one of the hundreds of millions of people who are joining the Internet. The only problem is that the computer industry has been there and done that. Instead, the future awaits in an entirely different direction, a place where expert systems will be much more specific and much less universal. (This does not in any way change the fact that if you can solve a problem for more people rather than fewer, you should naturally do it. But it should not be at the cost of producing a tool that performs much below the needs and expectations of the user.)

TRUTH, NOT OPINION

Just as the physician's first rule is to do no harm, the expert system's first responsibility is to remove error from the decision-maker's mind. Since the volume of available data is so extensively corrupted from so many sources (as shall be addressed in more detail in chapter 5), the existence of a reliable quality-control standard already greatly improves the accuracy of business decisions. The expert rules would create an array of gates to trap low-quality information and shunt it into delete space. Lies and misstatements would be explicitly sucked out and destroyed. And here again we hear the sceptics cry, "How can this be done?" though they have never even tried doing it.

But shall we say we live in a world where science is so stupid it cannot figure out what is a lie and what is not, cannot ascertain what is a misstatement of fact? Could not an expert system with appropriate categories of information simply check from an independent source that fact A is actually fact A? Could it not simply be a requirement that no decision-making process include assertions that are not attributed to an appropriate source? That rule alone would halt much business communication, where shouting unsubstantiated opinions is all too common. There is no reason to suppose it would be a programming nightmare to match a particular "fact" included in a message with the same "fact" recorded independently. This alone may not make clear which of the two is true, but any inconsistencies will be noted and invite resolution before the user takes action. There are well-understood, intellectually accepted tools that allow you to define the quality of information. Any university undergraduate is aware of them; they are contained within the general protocol for writing essays, for example. Indeed, we need simply take essay-writing rules and turn them into expert-system rules (that is, make them computable within a broader framework of information control).

While the quality of rules will vary depending on the subject matter, there are rules for every subject and some rules that are (or should be) common for all. Obviously, there will be different rules for, say, financial analysis and architectural design. The financial analysis will use more mathematical demonstrations, for example, while the architectural communication will make more reference to the principles of design. The absence of these types of information would alone be a quality "caution" flag. An architectural review of a building that makes no reference to the relationship of the building to its surroundings is, according to the weight of opinion of expert architects, a flawed set of observations. Equally flawed would be a publication that reflected no recognition of architectural scholarship, the work of other architects, new trends in design, and the needs of the buildings' users. Each of these attributes can be, and is, searched for using standard software systems.

Of course, users may not want to implement quality control on messages about their social arrangements or love life. But information for business purposes should not enter the user's mind until the expert system has reviewed it for accuracy. The goal continues to be that expert systems should save users time, so that they can think about those issues that actually require her attention. There is no reason for human beings to search citation references when it is so routinely a computable task and so easily orchestrated within a rule-bound framework.

INFORMATION AMOK

Expert systems will aid decision making because they overcome the otherwise horrific circumstance of there being too much to learn, too much to know.

Overcoming information overload is essential; if we don't, the promise of the information age will not be achieved. Unless the volumes of stored information can be properly managed and effectively accessed, social and economic value cannot be extracted. Although we're bombarded by information, we remain as ignorant as ever — or if the bombardment interferes with our learning, we end up even less knowledgeable. Yet even though information overload is often lamented, the responses to the problem are inadequate. Unfortunately, industry does not see this issue as urgent since most of its players operate under the same handicap and so relative competitive position is not affected.

Of course, when a better way to manage volume is finally developed, slow adoption would invite serious competitive disadvantage. It appears that industry does not always appreciate how overload interferes with its performance. The problem is more than the inability to find the key piece of data, to separate the relevant from the noise; there is also the impossibility of reading all the relevant information. But without all the relevant information, there is no certain way of knowing which questions to ask. And running throughout, there is a profoundly distracting babble in conflict with coherent thought. Understandably enough, many people, when facing such an apparently implacable and inevitable foe, respond by redoubling their efforts to focus, thereby inviting a kick in the head.

Every opportunity missed and every danger not averted lowers industry's rate of return. There is, therefore, a powerful incentive to address this problem, and the marketplace naturally waits for the information industry to provide a solution. It is proving to be a very long wait. Even though there are a variety of computer tools that search or filter information, they are fundamentally flawed from the perspective of industry. In many respects, this is not surprising. The information industry has a focus so narrow that many of the requirements of the business world are wholly unappreciated, and computing companies often misunderstand both their customers and their products. Information is so much more than writing code and moving megabits.

And there's another problem. Although the volume of stored digital data is vast, most of humanity's knowledge is not yet digitally stored. This has apparently not discouraged the many people who now use the Internet as their only information tool. If the information cannot be found on the Web, and quickly, these people believe, it does not exist. It would be difficult to imagine a more primitive idea.

While the exchange of meaningful information — communication — is important, the storage and organization of information should be equally important. Yet communication attracts a disproportionate amount of attention and resources, even though the total fund of humanity's information is of greater significance than the exchange of that information on any given day. This need is probably ignored partly because of the belief that storage is a routine and uninteresting problem. But any examination of this problem reveals layers of conceptually difficult issues, including those that go well beyond development. What should be added to storage? How should it be added? How should storage be organized? How can information in storage be accessed? These are just some of the inadequately explored issues.

Given the complexity, the subtlety, and the limitless nature of information, expert storage systems for specific fields of knowledge will prove to be indispensable. Users will not have to use a standard database to decide where things should go or how they should be categorized. Rather, the expert system will decide what database structure to use, what categories to use, what to include, how to include it, and whenever practical, how to extract it directly from the information flow and insert it into the relevant database. The fully developed rule system will also remind the user that additions to the database have been made, and that information that has now proved to be incorrect or irrelevant has been deleted. Of course, quality-control tools can also be sent into existing databases to purge them. Such self-adjusting databases, managed by expert systems, will provide solutions unique to particular industries without exhausting managerial time.

Let there be no doubt that this is a great challenge for those who wish to develop expert systems. It will take intensive research and experimentation to select the rules and determine the quality-control tools. At each step of the process, the expert system must rely on the scientific method. Where is the evidence? How much evidence is there? What is the state of human knowledge on this problem? What do we know that we are not applying? And those are only the opening questions.

THE NEVER-ENDING SEARCH

Without effective search engines, the promise of the Internet and the age of information cannot be achieved. In the vastness of the information domain, we must be able to find what we seek. And what we seek is meaning, not facts or data. The search for meaning is so great a challenge because we must look among an infinite array of possibilities. For any set of data, the number of meanings is unlimited because it is bounded only by the imagination of the observer.

Search engines have been built without anyone first studying volume in its own right; indeed, volume has not even been measured adequately. As a result, search engines are merely souped-up versions of yesterday's answer to yesterday's volume. After all, indexes and keyword searches are well-established techniques. Existing search engines are not even volume-robust; barely working at today's volume of information, they collapse at tomorrow's levels. Even now, most intelligent queries overload the user with more information than can be read. It is then suggested to the user that to defend against this overload, the query should be restricted or narrowed until the reading load is manageable.

This process is often called refining the query, but it actually means restricting it. And of course, at tomorrow's volume, the restriction must be even narrower.

In addition to revealing that search engines themselves do not guard against information overload, the suggestion to restrict the query is intellectually indefensible. The modification of a query should be driven only by the logical needs of the questions, not by the mechanistic dictates of software code. (Of course, poorly conceived questions should be refined or made more precise, but that is not relevant to a discussion about volume.) The only queries that can be effectively resolved using today's search engines are those to which the user already almost knows the answer. And next year, the user will have to be even closer to the answer.

Real questions are those to which the user has little idea of the answer. These are the questions whose answers drive the economy and its markets. They cannot be restricted to the degree required by the overload problem because there is no logical way to decide where the answer will *not* be found. Moreover, the more consequence the question has, the broader the query must be. In this sense, search engines, with their restricted questions, violate the most basic laws of intellectual inquiry, hardly an auspicious start to the age of information.

One alternative approach is to search using less rigid techniques, looking, for example, for "related" data according to a more general instruction. In other words, the search starts with a broader outlook. And that is certainly preferable to a search that is narrow at the beginning. However, these more general engines still provide more than can be read. And they must therefore screen (i.e., restrict) these findings to manageable levels. Most search techniques differ only in whether you narrow your search at the beginning or narrow the answers at the end. Either way, the effect of the restrictions substantially remains.

The better answer will be the expert search engine using expert databases. They will be built on the principles discussed in the next chapter.

CHAPTER FOUR

WORK,
NOT TALK

THUNDER OF A BILLION VOICES

The communications industry has achieved extraordinary prominence. It has spawned rich and powerful companies, made option millionaires out of many, and set off more than one stock-market stampede. Communication networks and infrastructure builders from AOL to Nortel to JDS Uniphase have had spectacular achievements. Their periodic difficulties merely attract more attention as they move through exaggerated cycles of boom and bust. Yet in spite of all of the limelight, their basic role is misunderstood. Away from the notoriety, another more powerful technology is gaining momentum.

The Internet as a personal communications tool is doomed to collapse unless expert systems ride to the rescue. And commercial opportunities on the Internet are equally at risk unless expert systems are developed for shoppers and buyers. The enemy is again volume: too many messages from too many places coming at you far too quickly.

There is, of course, no question that communication is the lifeblood of society and its marketplaces. We have known this for thousands of years — the ancient Romans knew it when they built the Western European road system and courier network, and Great Britain knew it when it instituted the penny post in the 1800s. It is equally clear that advances in the communication system, from the postal system and the telegraph to the telephone and the Internet, have facilitated both the exchange of information and economic activity. In other words, there appears to be a direct correlation between the ease of communication and the pace of economic activity. And it is so seductively easy to trend that relationship forward as a linear progression, even though it is not.

With the Internet offering a quantum reduction in the cost of computing, the volume of communication has exploded. The first law of communication — there is a direct inverse relationship between the cost of communication and the volume communicated — has been engaged. Because the cost of communicating on the Internet is almost negligible, we have experienced an expansion in volume that is effectively limitless.

For example, in 1999 e-mail use on AOL increased by 60 percent; the number of messages sent more than *doubled* from 1998. According to Ferris Research, the number of messages sent likely rose by more than 80 percent through 2000, and the size of the average message is expected to have increased by almost 200 percent. And there is yet no end in sight to this message growth.

The result is entirely predictable. No longer do rising levels of communication stimulate economic activity. At the very least, we have reached the stage where increased communication produces no stimulating effect at all. Indeed, as the volumes continue to rocket forward, driven by very low costs, there will soon be a negative effect on marketplace activity. The overall relationship between volume of communication and the stimulation of economic activity is not linear. Rather, it looks like the chart below — a relationship that rises to a peak and then relentlessly falls.

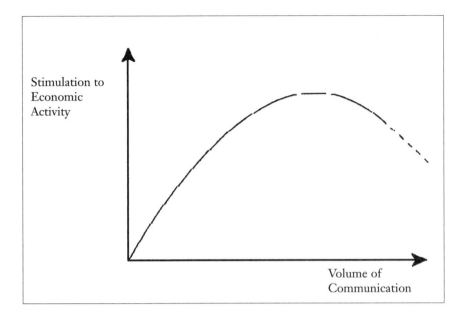

WHEN YOU HAVE A LIFE

Communication at this latter stage no longer aids decision making, economic activity, innovation, efficiency, or any other business concern. In fact, now the messages often impede decision making in one way or another. In some cases, decisions are slowed as the decision-makers try to digest all the information to which they are exposed; this produces decision making that is further and further behind the actual needs and conditions of the marketplace. In other instances, decision-makers attempt to cope by ignoring all messages, and therefore they do not receive the warnings that announce apocalypse now.

What is so easily forgotten in a discussion of the communications role of the Internet is how time-intensive the act of communicating actually is. Theories about the magical social effects of the Internet proceed on the blissful assumption that we already live in paradise, and that most people have enough time on their hands to surf, browse, chat, and engage in digital intercourse. But it is instructive to note that the most aggressive users of the Internet are those who have barely begun their lives. It is often assumed that the vast armies of teenagers and young persons cruising the chat rooms, browsing web site after web site, are there because they feel adept and comfortable with the technology. While this is perhaps partly the case, the essential truth of the matter is that they (and the elderly) are the ones who actually have time to engage in this feast of communication. Of course, teenagers and young people are also seeking companionship and information for their still quite empty minds. They seek stimulation and social and community connection. They are seeking a life, in effect, and seeking it through active communication is indeed not a bad plan. But they are not the principal workers of society.

By contrast, working adults in most of the industrial world — with their family responsibilities and friends (real friends in real places) — barely have time to talk to their children, never mind conversing with strangers halfway across the planet. Real persons with real lives have severe time constraints that grow progressively worse because of the competitive economy. Into this envelope of shrinking time availability, this black hole of communication time intrudes. The response is all too clear.

For those in business, the phone and the computer screen are now as much an enemy as an ally, an impediment as much as a productivity tool. This is not the case simply because each successive message offers less value than the one before it. (In other words, this is not just the law of diminishing marginal utility.) Rather, the volume is now so great that you have no idea whether the next message is of extraordinary value, no value, or so wrong it will sabotage you. You have no idea if the next message is vital or trivial. So on Tuesday, for example, the thirty-ninth message you receive is from your boss, telling you to respond at once to an irate customer; the fifty-first is another from your boss, reminding you about a retirement party for Joe, a person you have never met; and the fifty-second is from a person you do not know who is the CEO of potentially the largest customer you will never have (since you choose not to answer). What is happening more and more frequently in the face of this avalanche of messages is that people are simply disconnecting.

They do *not* queue the messages to reply to later — they merely delete them. This is the essential irony in the false dawn of the age of information. In the face of more information, many of us must retreat instead of advance, or just try to hold our ground.

If message volume was not enough of an impediment to business decision making and economic activity, the cheap cost of communication is producing a second and equal difficulty. The lower the cost of communication, the less time is spent in the composition of the message. Thus the second law of information — when communication is cheap and fast, you bang out the message that is at the forefront of your mind — takes effect. When you have a queue of one hundred messages you feel obligated to get through, you pound out responses, many of which are decisions or quasi-decisions. When you are a typical knowledge worker receiving more than a hundred messages a day — when you have to spend two, three, and sometimes more hours merely reading and responding to your e-mail — it is impossible to compose thoughtful replies.

It is instructive to note that the disappearance of personal letters written on paper has as much to do with time pressure as cheap telephone service. Therefore, it is quite easy to believe that, in all media, the amount of quality information exchanged is rising at a slower rate than the volume of communication. Indeed, the fear is that it might have actually declined. And the reason is so simple: the letter writer plans the communication as a special act, while the phone and e-mail are wondrously spontaneous (that is, chaotic and disjointed). An e-mail has the additional linguistic attribute of being blunt; it's communication with a sledgehammer.

The burden of message overload is much commented upon in popular conversation, in business discussions, and in the trade publications of the information industry. Often it is treated as one of those inevitable problems, like death and taxes. Overload carries with it the connotation that individuals must bravely soldier on in the face of arduous difficulties *over which they have little control.* This rather casual response again reflects a lack of thoughtfulness about the essential characteristics of information. It is all too easy to assume that technical connection is synonymous with communication. In other words, people confuse the simple act of logging on with the actual exchange of meaningful information. But having the ability to communicate — that is, the connection — by no means guarantees that the communication has occurred (or will occur), or that it will be a communication of correct information to explicit purpose.

This issue is certainly not about pushing more stuff down the pipe, and building a bigger pipe is hardly the answer (although it is to other matters). Startlingly enough in a marketplace where the lust for profit remains so strong, we would expect the difficulties of business communication to call out for improved software responses. This is especially so in a marketplace where each customer is so hard-won and fickle, where extra revenue is counted in cents but climbs easily to the tens of millions. Unfortunately, as is all too often the case, this subtle problem is left unaddressed while the macho war of pumping data has combatants aplenty.

When members of the IT industry are asked about communication overload, they readily acknowledge that it is a large, potentially great opportunity, a massive problem waiting to be solved. Yet even though they do not recognize it, their subsequent responses make clear how great the commercial opportunity actually is. In a response that is common to this industry, they assert that the solution to overload is either an as yet uninvented artificially intelligent agent or some simple coding. The middle-range answer, the development of a highly complex, rule-based expert system that would take great effort to create but is far from impossible, tends not to occur to them. (The basic logic of such a system is discussed below.) Thus they speak of this wonderful AI agent that will eventually read all your messages and decide what is important enough or interesting enough for you to want or need to see. We, of course, do not understand how or when such an agent will be created. And it is not immediately clear that it could tell you what you wanted or needed to know unless it could both read your mind and forecast the future.

PULLING UP THE DRAWBRIDGE

Alternatively, the user is directed to the filtering and screening tools that already exist for e-mail. But these systems are not expert. They do not work well because they cannot deal with rising volume, and they are in any event logically misconceived. Yet they do offer some value. It is certainly useful to keep off your screen the farm animal pornography site. It is useful and appropriate to screen out messages from people with whom you have chosen not to communicate. And plainly some people should have a higher-priority access to your mind, and thus their messages should automatically be queued to the top. That is a fairly straightforward programming function, and it already exists to a reasonable degree. However, this approach addresses so small a part of the overload problem as to offer no long-term potential. Such screening and filtering tools as currently exist are easily overtaxed by volume. But that weakness cannot make sense for any tool that is designed to deal with volume. The point is to have an instrument that is volume-robust; anything else is merely an interlude towards such a product.

If you take a filter and *make* it work to manage your message volume, then you have explicitly turned your back on the age of information (and incidentally, also on the Internet). The only way you can make a filter work in the face of the rising volumes of information is to narrow your personal portal into the communications networks. If you use a filter that allows only a known name to reach you, you will have no choice but to cut it off as soon as the number of known names reaches a particular limit. That is a problem that does not concern a teenager who hankers for more friends. But it is a deadly problem to any business decision-maker of even a moderate scope of responsibility. To produce an approved list of those who will be allowed access to you by virtue of who they are is no more than the beginning of the process of disconnection. And with rising volume, you will soon find yourself disconnecting some of the people who are already on your known list.

You could also, of course, filter by subjects, by categories in the headers, or by keywords in the text itself. You could, for example, instruct the machine to forward a message to you only if it includes one of sixty-two keywords. This will slow down the e-mail process, but since you are overloaded anyway, that is hardly a compelling objection. Unfortunately, this does not get us very far. As volume grows, your list of keywords will end up being restricted. It will shrink to thirty-two keywords from sixty-two, unless you decide you are going to spend a greater part of your day responding to e-mail. The choice is to restrict the list or do less work. But this is still essentially the response of disconnection. Instead of disconnecting yourself from everyone but those on your approved list, you are now disconnecting yourself from all the knowledge that cannot be subsumed in thirty-two keywords.

Let us remind ourselves why disconnection, the most common response to message overload, is so profoundly inappropriate and even, in a dynamically competitive world, dangerous. Disconnection means you cannot take advantage of society's new learning, new observations, new information, new insights, new anything. If you wish to guarantee that you will be blindsided in a dynamic world, draw a circle in the sand and say, "I shall not talk to anyone outside of this circle. I shall not think about any idea outside this subset. I have chosen to stay ignorant about everything else and about everybody else, except for what is in this exclusionary circle." There you stand, armed against the information overload of humanity, and your software screen does not note an imminent danger because you never thought of the possibility that a tidal wave would approach your picturesque cottage on the beach. You have guaranteed that unexpected information will never reach your mind until your feet are already wet.

While various kinds of filters and screens are currently available, they do not yet enjoy widespread use. One suspects that many people feel vaguely uncomfortable about using such an exclusionary tool; they fear, perhaps implicitly, that a nasty shock awaits them if they use what appears to be a rigid instrument. Instead, they opt to manage overload on their own, with whatever impulse happens to hit them that day. In other words, instead of becoming exclusionary, we simply become arbitrary.

The user is also often discouraged by how much work these filtering tools actually require. In addition to being awkward to use, these tools constantly have to be reinstructed. Even unsophisticated users will recognize that whatever screening constraints or criteria they set up will have to be modified on an ongoing basis. And that is yet another thing to do in an overcrowded workday. Such modifications will be especially difficult when users are not actually sure how to decide whether person A does or does not get to them. While it is easy to say the boss should always be able to get through to you, how do you decide about the thirty people who are sort of useful to you? Such decisions are neither easy nor quick to make, unless you explicitly decide to be arbitrary. This software is actually asking the user to make all the difficult decisions while it merely implements them. In other words, it's the opposite of an expert system.

There are, of course, some screening systems that try to learn the user's preferences. They adopt an approach similar to that used by software that helps people pick music or movies. In this case, the user indicates whether the message being received is appropriate or not, useful or not, and the software automatically tries to build an inventory using the characteristics of those messages ranked as useful. This has the virtue of allowing the users to evolve their own ideas of what is useful to them. This may also somewhat minimize the potential of being ambushed by a message you did not know to expect or ask for.

But from the user's point of view, the greatest obstacle to this more sophisticated approach is yet again that it takes time. Users must actually decide which messages are useful and which are not; they must, in other words, in the middle of a busy day, when they are hardly able to respond to the messages they already have, begin to characterize them. Is this useful to me? Is this not useful to me? I am not sure. I may not know for a week, or a month, or a year. Again and again, the software asks the user to do much more than there is time to do. In the paradise of unlimited time, it makes sense to spend a hundred hours learning a piece of software to save yourself a thousand hours of subsequent effort. If you only had the first hundred hours.

Given that it has never been more important to stay informed, and that the tools currently available do not even keep people connected, the commercial potential of an expert system for message management is great indeed. There should be a high return on any tool that dependably offers message mastery. But such an expert system has an even more important role to play, offering the besieged business manager and knowledge worker that precious resource: time. The expert system should not just "control" messages, squeezing message time into a finite block. Instead, it should offer you more information *with less use of time.* Who would not pay a premium for an extra hour in the day?

It will not be easy to create an expert program that harnesses the message flow of the Internet and other media, of course. It is amazing that anyone should think it would be. The critic may be tempted to ask how this could be done with programming that does not enter the domain of speculative artificial intelligence. But this is not the place to describe in detail the way such an expert system would work — for such a description would be a book in itself. After all, a better system for messaging management would require a complex set of rules, and it would take a long time to explain what those rules are and why they were chosen. But we can certainly describe the principal tasks that would be involved, none of which requires the use of anything other than established programming tools and approaches.

First, the system would prevent some messages from ever reaching your screen. In its simple form, the system would delete messages from any source — either a person or an organization — specified by the user. That means no more solicitations from the pornography sites, the bank, or your spurned lover. Then, as the exclusion list is added to by the user, an already well-established pattern-recognition program will look for common characteristics. It will note, for example, that the user rarely excludes individuals but almost always excludes commercial retail sites. In other words, the system will find rules to use to help it manage the messages. It can now take any new message that, while not explicitly excluded, meets the usual criteria of the excluded sources and place it at the bottom of the daily queue. The system is even quite capable of adding to its recognition pattern the fact that you always choose not to read the bottom of the queue, deleting all messages kept there sight unseen. That action by the user, of course, reinforces the pattern.

By contrast, if you choose to read the low-ranked messages, you will signal the system that its choices are "wrong."

However, even with a growing and responsive exclusion list, the number of messages can become unmanageable. So the second basic feature of this system is to organize and characterize the remaining messages. As before, the organizing criteria are specified by the user; at one level, this involves no more than computerizing what the users would do themselves if they had the time. That means no more screens with the mail listed in the order received. All messages from key senders (like the boss or the spouse) appear at the top of the queue. Less important senders are lower ranked and so on. Or the user can choose to rank messages based on subject headers (prioritizing, for example, any message with the subject heading "Sales"). Or the rankings can be organized by both sender and subject (a message from the boss about sales might get the top ranking). Additional criteria can be added by users depending on their particular situations. And here again, the system will look for common characteristics among higher-ranked messages and use those patterns to rank the messages that do not fit the pre-existing criteria. And by watching which messages the user actually reads or saves, the system can suggest new rankings or note that a present ranking appears ineffective. (Why is the vice-president of human resources highly ranked when the user reads this message last and usually deletes it without replying? There might be a good answer to that question, but the system serves the user by drawing attention to the apparent anomaly.) All this is possible without the user even looking at the content of the message.

By applying to message content search tools that measure word frequency and pattern recognition (not "spooky" AI), the system can draw inferences from the user's behaviour to suggest other priority criteria. For example, if the user normally responds with a long reply to any message that contains text words like "innovate," "new," "experimental," or "unconventional," the system will suggest prioritizing messages containing these words. Or perhaps the higher-ranked messages should be the ones that always contain financial data in the text. And as the user's behaviour changes, so too will these ranking criteria.

In addition, the system will deliver a full set of operating statistics. The user will be able to see at a glance how many messages arrive from specific places, concerning what subjects, and generating what replies. Trends over time will also be highlighted. It is, of course, impossible for the users to actively manage their personal communication flow unless they can describe it. Of course, the system will also use expert rules that have been drawn from independently conducted research about message-management practices, in addition to the particular user's behaviour patterns, to suggest alternative managing strategies or criteria.

It is critical to note that each of the above described steps is already performed to some degree by existing software. And while each step could be undertaken manually by the user, the possibilities for analysis are so great that the process easily becomes more than a human could or would do — which is exactly the domain of the expert system. Moreover, there are countless ways to manage messages that have not yet been discovered in this largely unexplored topic.

RULE HEAVEN

Expert systems find their rules in humanity's fund of knowledge, exactly where one would expect them to be. Admittedly, it is difficult to locate and extract these rules from all the other information that is, and pretends to be, knowledge. As a consequence, the expert system first must adopt rules about the management of information itself — that is, about how to organize, search, and apply information. In other words, expert systems must make rules about information in order to find the rules about everything else. The development of expert systems is thus dependent on the determination of information rules, a particularly challenging task. But it yields to the scientific method.

All of these information issues are *empirical* questions, and we can find the answers through scientific study. We have to make the study of information our highest priority, because until we understand information, the investigations into all other phenomena are impaired. Until we understand information in as many dimensions as possible, we will never be able to harness its power.

Where is the information coming from or going to? What are its types and characteristics? Are there multiple destinations? What are the internal and external dynamics of the flow of information? Are there tides and eddies, cross-currents and stagnant pools? How much like a river is information flow? In how many ways can it be configured or reconfigured? How can a database divide and subdivide again, yet remain whole? All these questions invite studied answers.

Expert developers need to make sure they have each question stated correctly. If necessary, they will have to restate the question to uncover the most insightful perspective. They shall draw on the most advanced scholarship with respect to all aspects of information. (These initiatives do not appear to be prevalent in many development companies, including those that dismiss expert systems as impractical.) They shall concern themselves with the exciting subjects of classification taxonomies and the variety of indexing procedures. But these subjects are truly exciting for those who would unleash the latent power of computing.

Classification systems provide an excellent illustration of how much logically straightforward study awaits and why it will produce actionable results. As the volume and diversity of information grow, new kinds of classifications and indexes become necessary. The diversity is a particular challenge, since as the subject matter proliferates, so do the number of sources and media of expression. Once upon a time, a category would be divided into one hundred subcategories; now it requires one thousand subcategories. And shortly, these subcategories will themselves have to be divided again. Any organizing system that continues that process indefinitely is sowing the seeds of its own destruction. In its most basic sense, classifying information is not an act of organization but rather an act of disassembly. It may be preparatory to organization and interpretation, but not when the information has been disassembled into dust.

Other forms of classification are also inadequate to the changing needs of research. Whether for business or academic purposes, whether pure or applied, research requires a much more intensive approach. More information or evidence is needed from more sources. More information must be extracted across classifications. And entirely new classes of inquiry are now receiving research attention. None of these trends will diminish.

Let's consider an example. Several decades ago, someone researching high blood pressure had to do no more than perform chemical experiments at a lab bench and read about other research in perhaps half a dozen scholarly journals. Now the stream of information relevant to the problem has become a tidal wave. Thousands of researchers are involved. Today's researcher must use search engines, read more, and visit scholarly web sites that use an entirely new method to contact others doing related work. In addition, since it is now understood that this disease is partly lifestyle-related, the researcher must follow the psychological research that tries to explain why people eat themselves to death, all drugs notwithstanding. And the drugs themselves are no longer created by simple trial and error; instead, they are designed molecule by molecule, which requires a deeper understanding of applied physics and biology. And since health-care expenses are soaring in the industrial world, most drugs now need to pass an economic cost-benefit test. This growing research complexity is not likely to stop in the foreseeable future.

Unfortunately, digital search engines have accidentally slowed the work in better classification systems. Because these engines can extract certain kinds of information very efficiently, they appear to reduce the need for classification. Information need only be stored in some digital code and a powerful search engine will find what you need, independent of the indexing system of the database. But that means that the indexing need not be done carefully or innovatively. This places all the burden on the searching procedure. Given the depth of the overload problem, that is more of a burden than the procedure can sustain (and as we've already seen, search procedures have their own limitations).

THE JOB OF ORGANIZATION

The existence of search engines has deflected attention from the need for research into storage organization. Yet several avenues invite further exploration. It should be possible to describe (tag) each specific piece of information with a variety of characteristics that reflect its form as well as its content. For example, each unit of stored information can be given tags (or labels) that, among other possibilities, describe its content, source, length, type (letter, memo, report, book), internal structure (summary, chapters, headers), composition (text, charts, numbers, photographs, art), citation history (how many times it has been used and by whom), popularity (growing or declining volume of output). These tags then become possible search criteria, as well as characteristics used to design databases. And as the nature of information changes — as different kinds and forms arise, as the volume in different subjects rises or falls — the storage formats and calibration tags will need to be updated and revised.

What is certain is that this new approach will place all the information precisely in the continuity of time, making it possible to analyze an event or a phenomenon over a period of years. Data-mining software, for example, looks at customer account files to see if there are associations that can be used to improve marketing. This might uncover the fact that a customer in a rural area buys particular types of products and therefore should be solicited separately. However, such analysis frequently uses just the most current records, ignoring the longer-term history of the customer. But information without continuity is uninterpretable, and when you mine in a timeless universe, your fate becomes a black hole from which neither you nor your analysis will emerge. Contrary to the popular impression, time-series analysis is meant for the entire life sequence of the event, not just the past quarter or year. And if the life of the event is longer than the record (as is too often the case), you will be able to at least try to recreate the lost records. Of course, all the laws of intellectual inquiry are violated if the only information you use is that which is already available. "That's all there is" is the excuse of an intellectual flathead.

We should not be deflected even for a moment by the comment

that such historical analysis is a lot of work. Of course it is. But if the alleged age of information means anything, it means the intensive use of information. It means more people using more information for more purposes. It means less ignorance. It does not just mean more computing. It does not mean more half-baked, one-dimensional pseudo-solutions.

The difficulties faced in the struggle for an informed society can clearly be seen in the state of many of the world's digital databases. Most cannot provide any time-series capability. This is partly because the design of the systems does not allow a sort by time in any practical sense. Some databases actually destroy "dated" information, making time-series impossible. Such acts of barbaric vandalism naturally occasion little comment in our dark world.

While digital storage is convenient and cheap, and offers some superior characteristics, paper libraries and archives also have advantages. For mass storage, a real warehouse can still be cheaper than disk space. And since throwing out records takes physical effort, and there is often no practical way to sort "useful" information from "useless," entire sets of records are often kept "just in case." Inefficient, say those of limited perspective; let us computerize information so it is easy to delete. But what is made easy is easily done in thoughtless hurry. The historian is, of course, appalled. The problem is that there is no assured way to know what will be useful in the future, even if you have enough information to know what is useful now. Indeed, some companies decide what records to store simply by learning whether the law requires their storage. What makes tax regulations relevant to intellectual inquiry defies answer. Or does business think that management does not require intellect?

The physical library also has the advantage that even the less informed tend to be made uneasy by the sight of books in a dumpster — or even worse, in flames. Of course, striking the Delete button produces no such reaction. But this makes things too easy to scrap, and so the expert system for information organization will make deletion from storage possible only with high-level approval and a built-in delayed response.

Another essential characteristic of an appropriately organized database will be that each significant element of information will be linked internally to other relevant elements. To avoid misinterpretation based on an incomplete search for information, the database will automatically offer links to the user. However, these links will be more than the result of a search engine looking for connecting threads; rather, they will arise from the intellectual organization of the database, thus presenting connections that should be made but often are not. Presumably, this process would naturally follow from the basic database structure. By preventing information from being offered out of context, this feature will become indispensable to any organization that wishes to develop an effective decision-making process.

There are, in fact, many avenues for improving structural characteristics. This is a direct result of the fact that organization is not one of the more glamorous aspects of computing. However, placing a piece of information in its correct context and continuity (out of tens of thousands of possibilities) is a computing application of high degree. The inability of search engines to compensate for overload in most circumstances will be corrected only when improved engines work in collaboration with improved databases, with both search engine and database designed with the other in mind.

LET SCIENCE RULE

Search engines themselves will not be significantly improved until the focus of attention is on the user and the user's needs. These needs are not easily described, even by experienced researchers themselves (on the rare occasions when they are consulted). As a result, the researcher can obtain answers to only very narrow questions. The rest of the search task, 99 percent of it, remains the responsibility of the researcher, with the software itself offering only supplemental assistance. Part of the difficulty is that many software developers have an understandable difficulty imagining complex queries or queries containing a series of specific questions contingent on previous answers. The possible query pathways can easily spin into the thousands.

We are limited by our poor knowledge of how higher-level queries are formed (and equally important, how they *should be* formed). It is somewhat startling to observe that one response to the absence of this understanding is AI's determined attempt to mimic generalized human thought processes, about which we know even less.

Expert developers will also use those other scientific standbys: experiment and observation. Innovations are not created by asking people what they want; this is only a starting point for your own line of investigation. With radical innovations, people do not know what to ask for because, after all, they are not the innovators. It takes imagination to know what you want because you actually have to describe what could be created. Users are rarely able to do so. Instead, expert developers ask users what they are doing with information and what their problems are, without asking for the solutions. And they ask a scientifically representative sample of users. Of course, such a representative survey is expensive, since it asks many questions and must be prepared to accept many kinds of different answers.

Moreover, it will also be necessary to observe the users, since many people cannot describe what they are doing, do not have the time to describe what they are doing, and often misdescribe what they are doing. Therefore, developers who are serious about expert systems will engage in lengthy and direct observation of users in the widest possible range of situations. This is undoubtedly a huge effort, and it challenges the software industry to advance beyond the domain of technician into the role of observant scientist. It should not be a role that appears inappropriate or inconsistent, since most degrees in computing are in what is called (perhaps idealistically, but quite correctly) computer *science*. The observations that result from this lengthy and expensive process will provide the fuel to generate hypotheses. In this particular context, the hypotheses are about rules. And while intellectually and imaginatively challenging, the task is really quite simple. Will this rule help the users find the information they want or need? Will this rule help them turn information into meaning?

Once the hypotheses have been formulated, the expert developers will test them. They will test them with representative samples of users, not on themselves. They will not decide that *they* like the interface. They will not decide that *they* like this rule over that one. They will test the rules with users in real situations and observe the results. Drug companies, for example, do not test the hypothesis that drug X will lower blood pressure by administering it to one person and asking him whether he feels better. The computer industry is surely ready to apply the scientific method to the pursuit of an effective solution, rather than to the execution of a software solution.

When these observations are offered to a group of professional and experienced developers, their reactions are on occasion somewhat disconcerting. They tend to wonder exactly what rules would create an expert system for information management. That question alone is interesting because it implies that one should be able to think up these rules on the spur of the moment. But the point is that you cannot do so. This is a complex problem, and it will be answered only with genuine research, costly and uncertain though that may be.

It is thus clear that in the beginning, this degree of information research will be feasible only for those commercial ventures where the danger of loss is very high or the lure of profit very strong. The financial industry, which is about nothing more than information, is the most likely candidate. It already conducts some aspects of this research, and the industry understands full well that a small but critical piece of information can make or lose billions in the space of days. The pharmaceutical industry is another where the ability to command great volumes of complex data buys wealth (and for proprietary drugs, monopoly power).

Those in the information industry itself will also be able to bear the cost of intensive information research. While they would prefer not to, they will have little choice. Only by moving in this direction can they create the next generation of profitable products. Today's software, Internet and all, has just about run its course.

CHAPTER FIVE

VOID OF IGNORANCE: WHERE ANGELS FEAR TO TREAD

THE ARGUMENT THAT DARE NOT SPEAK ITS NAME

The vastness of society's ignorance is the principal reason why expert systems have such potential, *and* why they can be reliably created with today's technology. Since most people are ignorant about most things, it is easy to assume that many of these gaps in knowledge can feasibly be corrected. The ignorance spans such an enormous range that there are many examples of high-priority problems that can be resolved with relatively small amounts of accurate data. The stock market would not have lost trillions of dollars in value in 2000 and 2001 if investors had simply known what is taught in any good secondary school course in introductory economics: profit counts, and rising interest rates lower profit. Sunbeam's investors would have saved themselves if they had known what the senior executives did about the strange behaviour of their CEO, Albert "Chainsaw" Dunlap. Olympia and York's managers would not have destroyed the once huge property developer if they had merely *listened* to the Federal Reserve Board in the late 1980s. Barnes and Noble would be the world's undisputed king of the booksellers if it had only *noticed* the Internet before Amazon.com. Children's lives could have been saved if their physicians had known how slowly the brain dies when a child has *almost* drowned in freezing water. The list goes on.

There must also be complex problems that remain unsolved solely because we are ignorant of the various elements that could produce a solution. The worst fear of cancer researchers is that they already have all the pieces that need to be put together to find a cure, but that the final link lies unread in an obscure journal. As evidence, we need only note the decades that Barbara McClintock's insights into genetics lay unused, or even the time it took to recognize that nerve cells can regenerate. The evidence for repeated and catastrophic comet impacts on earth was available long before someone saw the connections that led to this conclusion.

While it is often assumed that every unsolved problem *cannot* be solved with today's knowledge and technology, the evidence to substantiate this belief is utterly absent. Just because you have not heard of the answer does not mean that it does not exist. If we were already using almost all the knowledge to which we have access, and quickly learned to use all new information as it became available, the market for expert systems would be no more than a modest niche. The presence of ignorance, however, belies that conclusion.

Of course, the documentation and analysis of social ignorance is an awkward exercise. If you point to the ignorance of society, you paint yourself as the embodiment of arrogance. Decry ignorance and you are labelled an elitist snob, accused of treating with condescension those you take to be fools. Emphasize the ignorance and you are accused of seeing everyone but yourself as a dullard. This is truly the argument that dare not speak its name. Of course, this does not make the argument false, just difficult to articulate.

Research into expert software begins with an intensive and continuing analysis of information in its own right. Until this research is fully engaged, the age of information is no more than a vague promise. Of course, to study information is to study ignorance, especially the ignorance that results in unsolved problems. Ignorance is a central fact of human existence and a sombre backdrop to the computing industry. Ignorance shapes every aspect of the information technologies, and computing cannot be fully understood except as a means to address this void. By "ignorance," we mean not just the absence of information, but also the presence of incorrect information.

You may find it easy to accept this argument when you think of how ignorant other people are. Yet this reaction does not do justice to the degree of ignorance that exists. Society's ignorance is both profound and pervasive, and none of us is exempt. It is not just that a few pieces of information get past us, not just that a professional's information base is a bit too narrow, not just that millions of people read supermarket tabloids, not just that tens of millions of people watch lies on television, not just that most people cannot describe the main historical events of their society, not just that most people cannot explain how a photocopier works or understand a weather forecast, not just that most people do not have the vocabulary to describe the complexities of the world — no, it is much more.

It is about educated degree-holders who cannot say anything accurate, never mind perceptive, about any subject beyond their area of specialization, who instead trumpet headlines and folklore as fact. It is about environmentalists who have their science backwards and imperil the planet they are attempting to save. It is about teachers whose misinformation leads their students astray. It is about students who choose careers they cannot accurately describe. It is about media coverage that is so contradictory as to be incoherent. It is about businesspeople who plunge into markets that an hour of research would have shown to be non-existent. It is about lawyers who do not know the law and physicians who know less than their patients. And it is about the legions of consultants whose only expertise is their ability to shape mountains of words into castles of glib illusion.

It is tempting to believe that this argument exaggerates the ignorance of society, and certainly our own ignorance. But consider the evidence. When polling organizations ask almost any question that has a factually correct answer, respondents typically get it wrong. So much of the public thinks that crime is rising when it is falling, that employment levels are falling when they are rising, that ethnic group A (pick any one) is made up of laggards or thieves, that sexual activity is debilitating, that the president of the United States has power, that lenders want their money back, that foreign trade is bad, that irradiated food is radioactive, that Detroit was never invaded, and that aliens are watching us. Indeed, from society's point of view, no event is too trivial to notice, no issue too significant to ignore, no idea too stupid to believe, no positions too contradictory to hold, no fad too foolish to follow, and no body of evidence too heavy to reject.

The ignorance of society is so pervasive that it is often not even noticed; indeed, we cannot even define what would constitute a knowledgeable citizen. No thought has been given to applying to a representative sample of adults a standardized test of "knowledgeability" similar to those now aggressively recommended for school-aged children. There could hardly be any doubt of the results. In fact, there is no definitive and comprehensive measurement for public knowledgeability at any level, for any age. And even though computing now gives us the capability to create one, no one has dared try.

BEDLAM IN THE MARKETPLACE

Ignorance in business is, of course, punished by the marketplace, and those who doubt the scale of ignorance should note the magnitude of those repeated punishments. Year after year, bankruptcies arise from the same mistakes. Losses short of bankruptcies bleed untold billions from society's wealth. Resources that earn less than their best potential reward starve more fruitful opportunities and add to the weight of disadvantage. Yet all the wreckage is blissfully marked down to the imperfections of human nature and the uncertainties of life, not to the ignorance that could, and *should*, have been corrected. This warm and soft excuse is offered without, as usual, any evidence to support it.

It might be argued that this critique of business knowledgeability is unfair, nothing more than armchair quarterbacking. Losses occur, after all, because of the complex unpredictability of the marketplace, and certainly some losses are honest errors in judgement. But this cannot be true in many cases, especially given the ignorance so many business-people demonstrate about the factors that can make them successful. Their understanding of specific marketplaces is often primitive or absent. Their knowledge of the broader economy is often wrong. Business-people routinely fail to correctly identify their competitors or well-established market trends. This is why the long-established auto industry fails to understand the importance of quality, the trend towards falling international trade barriers, or the marketability of design. IBM misses the personal computer. Retail giants ignore the Internet until Amazon.com appears out of nowhere to startle them into action. Whether it's demographics or credit conditions, businesspeople act on impressions, instead of facts. During the 1990s, a successful book by David Foot and Daniel Stoffman, *Boom, Bust & Echo*, held the attention of tens of thousands of readers as it described the importance of the post-war baby boomers in the marketplace. Obviously it was of use to those readers, even though it did no more than draw attention to a demographic trend that had existed for *decades*, and had already been much commented upon by others. Yet apparently it was necessary to tell people that it is helpful to count consumers and to count them by age.

Growing firms, whether small or large, tend to have clear and impressive areas of expertise. The marketplace normally guarantees that a minimum level of knowledge is necessary for continued growth. However, even larger and growing enterprises tend to have a knowledge base that is narrow in comparison with what they need to know. Outside of their core technology or marketplace, their knowledge quickly turns to mush. And that is why so many large and successful corporations run aground in the space of a few years, wondering all the while what hit them. How can IBM, in a relatively short span of time, go from being an allegedly all-powerful monopoly to living in Microsoft's shadow? How can Chrysler be an attractive takeover target one minute and a basket case a year later? How did Sears lose its retail dominance? How did AT&T, the mighty telephone system, so lose its way that it ended up overshadowed by almost all the telcos in America? What happened, of course, is that each one of these companies was hit by a new development one millimetre outside of its line of vision. And it was often a new development that had already attracted much comment and discussion. In other words, they could have known but did not. (It has also been argued that some of the failings of business are the result of executives who do not have the courage to act, even when they know what they should do. This is difficult to judge, since ignorance is so commonly encountered.)

If most executive decisions were made on a truly knowledgeable basis, then there would be very few sudden changes in direction or perception. Knowledge, as scholars will tell you, is won only slowly. It is not a statement of knowledge to say first that Japan is about to take over the industrial world and then that its financial system is collapsing; that Korea is hot and then is not; that derivatives are good, then bad, then good again; that robotic factories are productive and then they are not; that oil is going to be a hundred dollars a barrel and then it is not; that mergers are great and then they are not; that diversification lasts until we return to core functions; that employees are empowered until they need to be knowledge workers; that stocks are up and then they crash. And on it goes, rushing from one idea to the next with no time for thought or consideration. This is plainly decision by momentum, and the business community exhibits such herd-like behaviour so often as to make lemmings look like free thinkers.

The surest indicator that many economic losses could be avoided if we used the knowledge already available to us is the extent to which mistakes are repeated, as generation after generation goes over the cliff. Ask sophisticated investors how many times corporations make the same mistake. Ask lending officers that same question. Ask them why so many new businesses fail and listen to them cite the same three reasons: poor management, poor marketing, and insufficient capital. The last two North American real-estate fiascos were merely one spectacular example of persistent error. We built buildings because everyone was building, even though we should have known what a recession induced by restrictive monetary policy does to real-estate value. If we did not know that in the early 1980s, we surely knew it in the 1990s, correct? Apparently not. But maybe this is no surprise. After all, many executives would be hard pressed to describe with any degree of accuracy the monetary history of the past several decades, even though any competently taught eighteen-year-old economics student could do it.

The stock-market fiasco that opened our new century could be described as many things — except surprising. It can't be considered a surprise that interest-rate increases inevitably slow economic activity, that slower economic activity forces down profits, that the tech sector is not isolated from the overall economy, that companies without business plans or logic fail, that price-earnings ratios have an upward limit of rationality, or that technology plays are riskier than well-established enterprises. Nor could there have been any doubt that the scent of fear in the air would send the herd into full-blown panic.

Business executives, of course, claim that they base their decisions on facts, on evidence. But if that were true, how do we account for the fact that most major corporations do not have a scholarly archive that documents and analyzes their past history? Why are the corporate histories that do exist mainly written by journalists, not historians? Why do you rarely hear senior executives making clear statements about the lessons they learned from the history of their companies or their industries, or from history itself? Why would any rational business executive say, as some have, that a knowledge of company history would be "constraining"? The "let's be creative with nothing in our head" argument belongs in kindergarten, not the boardroom.

The argument that markets are efficient because they quickly use all available information is both true and false. Markets tend to "price in" all the information its participants have, so they are efficient in that narrow technical sense. And while incorrect information is driven out of the market over time, there is often a continuing misinformation loss, with one incorrect piece of information being replaced by a different inaccuracy. Moreover, since the markets do not include in their calculations all the relevant information known to society, their decisions are inherently inefficient according to the most basic laws of economics (because resources are not being applied to their best possible use).

A LITTLE LEARNING

Admittedly, over the course of the twentieth century, public ignorance has declined, albeit slowly. Mass literacy and public education have in fact lowered the state of ignorance from abysmal to merely very great. And as educational levels continue to increase, the level of ignorance will fall. But several qualifications apply. Formal education provides no more than expertise in a very narrow band; there is little emphasis placed on integrating diverse information, even when it is known. (These observations do not assume that educational standards have declined over time; the evidence for this decline is questionable, with areas of decline probably balanced by new areas of knowledge.) The narrowness of contemporary education means that when it comes to broad areas of knowledge, the educated person is not much better off than anyone else. The best that can be said is that educated people are a bit less ignorant than their unschooled colleagues.

The news media do add to public information, at least across a small class of current events and social issues. When there is a single public event, like an earthquake or an assassination, the media contribute to a more knowledgeable society. As well, they can dependably inform society about a straightforward issue (by telling people, for example, that unprotected sex invites AIDS). But the more complex the issue, the less effectively the media disseminate information. How can we expect them to explain why poverty is so hard to eliminate, why child abuse occurs, how to solve global warming, or even whether it is a true problem? Viewers do not seem to want *any* story to last more than thirty seconds, and readers do not want more than a couple of paragraphs. Indeed, the proportion of households that read newspapers is in decline. In such circumstances, it is difficult to imagine how the media could do better, especially when "headline" media continue to draw viewers from more in-depth coverage. And of course, since history is not news, and therefore is not "interesting" to many people, context and continuity are presented mainly by accident. Hence much of what passes for news has elements that confuse rather than inform.

Even though media outlets struggle to report complex matters, we all tend to defer to them. But do lawyers trust the media to report accurately on legal issues? No, although they still trust them on every other subject. Businesspeople know the media mangle business issues, but they trust them on political matters. Politicians know the media fail to communicate the essential complexities of public policy, yet they trust them on scientific issues. And scientists often laugh when they read the media's description of physical phenomena, yet they trust their characterizations of the economy.

On the subject of the economy (a principal influence on the life of everyone on the planet), the media inevitably produce such a stew of incomplete and out-of-context observations as to make any systematic observation impossible. They report the unemployment rate, even though it cannot be interpreted without the employment rate; they confuse debt levels with ongoing deficits; they report debt levels without concomitant asset figures, and so defy high-school accounting standards; they avoid time series for fear that too many numbers are boring; in the name of balance, they report lunatic screeds that repudiate evidence and logic. And they do so not out of malice, but out of the ignorance and bias of those they report on. In this sense, the media portray very accurately the society of which they are a part.

Then there is electronic entertainment that celebrates outright stupidity and gratuitous violence. So-called reality TV tells us more about the state of general reality than we might wish. Worst of all are those entertainments that purport to be fact or pseudo-fact (so delicately called "speculations"); these actively mislead millions, and defend themselves by saying, "It could be true." Precious airtime is devoted to "investigations" of hauntings, aliens, ancient predictions, conspiracies, killer bees, witches, werewolves, monsters, incantations, and publicity-seeking dysfunctional families. They are at war with the scientific method, and they are winning too many battles.

So even as more people become better educated, part of that benefit is cancelled by the carelessness of the media and the irresponsibility of the entertainment industry. Just as someone new graduates from high school, someone else is reading a tabloid in the grocery line. The entertainment industry says that it just gives consumers what they want, what makes a profit in a market economy. But this is the classic vicious circle: the public is too ignorant to know how poorly it is served, and the entertainment industry is no smarter than its customers. And so they dance together in the darkness, with the news media doing no more than holding an intermittently flickering candle.

RUN FASTER . . . FALL FARTHER BEHIND

The most compelling problem is not absolute ignorance, however, but rather relative ignorance: the proportion that you do not know of what you need to know. Of course, the volume of what anyone needs to know to function in the contemporary world is increasing rapidly, and this increase shows no sign of abating. Global competition continues to drive up the standards of performance in all work situations, as well as the standard of knowledgeability. Advances in technology add their own demands for more expertise. And if that were not enough, the complexities of modern society proliferate.

In the past, all you had to know about financial advancement was to save your money and deposit it in a bank, about career was to find a good employer and stick with the company, about marriage was to get someone to say yes, about children was to feed and clothe them, about sex was to do what came naturally, and about your health was to eat peas once a week. Today, any of these behaviours can invite personal disaster. Tomorrow they may guarantee it.

While the need for knowledge is increasing rapidly, there is no evidence to suggest that knowledgeability is growing at the same rate. Indeed, there is some evidence that it is emphatically not, as public literacy declines and some scores on standardized school tests erode. The only conclusion that can reasonably be reached is that the degree of relative ignorance is actually increasing.

It seems clear that many people do not know enough about how to do their work most effectively or how to fully achieve their personal goals. What each individual needs to know varies, but the fact that many of us are falling behind our need to know is undeniable. While we can at least function (for a while yet), the real issue is how far from our potential we are. The consequences of this mounting ignorance run counter to the age of information, and can only increase the likelihood of every kind of social and economic mistake. And in an age that does not seem to worry about ignorance, perhaps it needs to be said that ignorance hurts. It hurts us individually and collectively, immediately and over the long term. It hurts across the entire range of our lives. And it invites the chance of catastrophic failure.

IN THE LEAKY BOAT TOGETHER

A more thoughtful approach might note that this is an argument about *society's* ignorance, in which we all share. We do not know as much as we should. Indeed, today we know a smaller proportion of what we need to know for our personal success than we did last year. We should feel ourselves being sucked into a black void. What is difficult to understand is why society does not recognize these concerns. To be blind to your own ignorance and that of others is the real arrogance. Why do some who see the ignorance underestimate its extent? Why do those who see its extent fail to feel the urgency to act? Why does the computer industry seem oblivious to its central challenge: to vanquish this ignorance and improve the quality of decision making.

The answer lies partly in the confusion between humanity's fund of knowledge and public ignorance. The stock of what is known and stored in libraries has never been greater, and it continues to rise rapidly. But this is not knowledge in action, because it is not widely known. We must remind ourselves that information is useful only when it is known and acted upon. The degree of that usefulness is determined by the number of people who know and act.

Another part of the answer lies in the fact that we do not live in a society that truly loves learning; a society that is determined to learn as much as it can and to make sure that everything it knows is true; a society where this determination is deep and steady, affecting every aspect of human life; a society that revels in the pure joy of learning. Instead, as has always been the case, most of us apply learning to bits and pieces of our lives, often with little thought of connection. We learn what we need to know to make a living; we learn golf or cooking because it gives us pleasure. And even much of this limited learning is done with no particular passion (except possibly for golf).

Indeed, much of what passes for learning is more the receipt of established knowledge than it is a process of critical examination (without which learning cannot truly be said to have occurred). The steadfast use of the scientific method, the test of logic and evidence, is often lacking in our schools, never mind in the rest of society. And even teachers who apply it in one domain forget to apply it in another. So in spite of the rhetoric we hear about education, knowledge workers, and the age of information, learning today is marked more by its absence than by its presence. For a person profoundly in love with learning, today's world is a dark and primitive place where there are only a few islands of understanding in a sea of superstition, rumours, lies, confusion, trivia, and every kind of error of fact and logic. The dawn of the twenty-first century is figuratively but a few minutes past the Middle Ages, as anyone with historical perspective should know.

Advocates of the Internet expect the mere existence of the network to usher in an age of enlightenment. But that would happen only if we already lived in an intellectual paradise. The absence of the love of learning explains why the Internet is such a modest tool to use to overcome ignorance. To those who love learning, the Internet can be an efficient tool to do research, conduct dialogue, and share insight. But for those who do not have a passion to learn, the Internet is of little or no value. Only those who love learning love libraries. To suggest that the "convenience" of the Internet will induce those people who are already too lazy to go to their local public libraries to acquire information defies common sense. To render information useful, accessibility is a necessary but not sufficient condition.

Indeed, the ignorance of society is on proud display on the Internet. In many ways, it is a salute to the repudiation of logic and the celebration of paranoid stupidity (in addition to every depravity known to humanity). Moreover, in a society already pressed for time, it has replaced television as the greatest thief of time. It wastes the time of those who are seduced by it and of those who devote their lives to web sites of neither consequence nor reality. Do we really need to know who did what to whom in a long-dead situation comedy? Even the efficiency of the Internet as a research tool is compromised by the number of idiots who appear on your screen in spite of your best efforts to avoid them. But most significant and dangerous of all is the ability of the Internet to communicate the howl of the mob and the incitement of a demagogue with a speed and breadth heretofore unknown. Now stupidity can envelop the globe in seconds. And because the Internet is so cheap, any fool can have a podium and a potentially wide audience. Rather than replacing one stupidity with another, the Internet gives each one a presence in the planet's electronic consciousness.

There are several reasons why we have only the rhetoric of learning and not the reality. There are those who are too lazy or too disorganized to exert themselves, and in the society of the unlearned, they can get by; there are those who have never tasted the joy of learning, or have tasted it in no more than a thin gruel; there are those who try to learn but, in a society hostile to learning, are stymied at every turn. The relentless pressures of society demand action, not reflection, and the tired mind cannot learn even when a fleeting moment presents itself.

Time constraints are the great enemy of learning. There is hardly time to hug a child, much less time to read (still the most effective way to program the human brain). The alternative, listening and watching, is demonstrably inadequate for any higher-order skill, from engineering to business. A businessperson wishing to be even minimally informed about the context of business (not even the specifics of a particular business) would have to read at least one daily local newspaper, one daily business newspaper, one weekly news magazine, and several business periodicals — a reading load that adds up to at least eight hours a week. And we must not forget ten minutes a day scanning the electronic news media. That is merely the beginning of the week's learning responsibility.

THE DIGITAL DIVIDE

The computing industry, in exquisite irony, exhibits the most frenzied atmosphere of any industry. The pace of competition and the shortness of the product cycle appear to guarantee this (even though the other approach to competition is to use proprietary technology to create true "killer" applications, products serving a demand that is both high priority and long term). As a consequence, computing itself is often unable to offer an environment conducive to learning. That is, of course, why the industry needs its gurus, people who divine the future from the perspective of n-space.

The question to be asked is whether computing can fundamentally contribute to a more learned society. It will not do so simply by the creation of a mystical "digital" community; it will also not do so just because of digital storage or transmission, and certainly not because of speed. Increased computing power is also not the answer. But computing may break the cycle of an ignorant society because of its one overriding characteristic (a characteristic that has, as we have seen, already substantially transformed society): it is cheap. Communication is also cheap. And both are getting cheaper, with no end apparently in sight.

Low cost is not the answer itself, but it allows the creation of practical tools to challenge ignorance in new ways and to help users make more knowledgeable decisions. Unfortunately, society does not yet fully appreciate the need for computer-generated experts. After all, it has human experts and expertise. But this fund of expert knowledge is often not known or used. Cheap computing in the form of the expert system can mobilize *and* mandate knowledge. The expert system dissipates ignorance by placing knowledge directly in the face of the user and insisting upon its use. Alternatively, the system makes the decision itself. In either event, the knowledge is in use and fewer ignorant responses occur. For the moment, there is a failure to see the expert system as an answer to general ignorance. But when that log-jam is broken, the market will sweep aside anyone or anything in its path.

Those members of the computer industry who do understand that information is more than a commodity are waiting until enlightenment dawns, and then they intend to cobble together an imitative response. Unfortunately for them, that tactic (it can hardly be called a strategy) will not work. Programming for obvious solutions can be duplicated with reasonable ease. But ignorance-busting, category-making expert software cannot be so easily reproduced.

Still, many of those in the old school of computing are of the same mindset as the majority of those in the entertainment industry: they do not expect enlightenment ever to appear in the mass market. They believe that the ignorant will always be with us. Indeed, when we look at the information industry, it is difficult to find reasons to conclude that a majority of its participants actually believe in the value of accurate information, never mind knowledge or wisdom. There certainly is little action to suggest they do. But a few companies and individuals do see knowledge as the ultimate application, and they are developing systems to improve decision making for engineering design, customer relations, information management, and health care. From the seeds they are planting, a social and economic transformation will grow.

HOW DEEP THE SWAMP

The surest sign of the primitive state of the information industry is its failure to study its adversary. The word "study," in this sense, means rigorous analytical research and precisely defined quantitative measurements. The extent of ignorance cannot be determined with studies of a few unrepresentative focus groups laid on top of the trend lines of some existing products. And research is certainly not asking the ignorant what they do not know.

There are presently no credible comprehensive benchmarks of society's ignorance. The absence of these measures slows down all of the information industry, most particularly computing. If public research into this topic was available, product development would be dramatically accelerated. The lack of attention paid to ignorance by university-based researchers again reflects the low priority society assigns to learning, even within the institutions that should be at the forefront. Of course, to study this topic, the university researchers would first need to see themselves as part of the herd of the ignorant.

However, in the absence of publicly available information about ignorance, an absence that will last for some time, companies that do their own proprietary research can gain a significant competitive advantage. They will find the openings for new expert systems, the places where expert rules are just waiting to be put into play. At a basic level, the process is straightforward. For example, a routine investigation would uncover the fact that engineers generally know very little about marketing, even though it is obviously true that the products they design must sell. That observation alone is not enough to tell a developer how to create an expert system to help engineers, but it suggests an opening to be explored. Further investigation would reveal that in the business world, the engineer's lack of marketing expertise is, if even recognized, addressed only by having the marketing department "oversee" the design process. But this oversight frequently fails to be effective, for any number of reasons, from the organizational barriers that keep marketing and design in separate kingdoms to the marketing managers' lack of understanding of the design process (a separate knowledge deficiency). In other words, there is a persistent and important problem that occurs because of a lack of information among an identified group of people in an identified situation. Since the basic principles (or rules) of marketing are well established, the opportunity for an expert system logically beckons.

However, if the developer wants an expert system that works very well

— so well that it is welcomed by all parties, can command a premium price, and cannot easily be duplicated by others — a further documentation of ignorance is necessary. An expert program that just generically tries to teach an engineer all the basic marketing principles is not likely to do justice to the topic, and the engineer is not likely to have the time to be "taught." (And there is little likelihood of proprietary insight.) The goal of the expert system is always to save time *and* improve the quality of the work.

Therefore, further research is needed to determine exactly what aspects of marketing knowledge the engineer must know to improve the design process. The answer is not that he needs to know "everything" about marketing, an impossible and unnecessary standard. Rather, the development team searches for high-leverage elements of marketing knowledge that can produce dramatically better designs. Such elements are also likely to be highly dependent on the circumstances of the work — the nature of the products being designed, the industry, the market conditions for this category of products, and the particular design process itself. Thus the expert marketing aid for a chemical engineer is likely to be different from that for an electrical engineer.

Those on the expert development team will be able to create such effective solutions because they will have an intimate understanding of the customers and their problems (a key marketing rule itself). They use this superior knowledge to select the most important rules, shape and sequence them for the greatest effectiveness and efficiency, and meld them into a seamless part of the design process. It is a solution possible only because the developer has taken the measurements carefully.

While the measurement process is lengthy and uncertain (because you will never know what you will find), the logic is straightforward: document the things that people do not know that adversely affect their work performance, then create a specific tool to fill the knowledge gap. The danger is that the research can be overwhelmed by the scope of our collective ignorance.

With a few exceptions, the developers will not have the resources to conduct comprehensive open-ended measurements, and as a result, the research will have to be carefully targeted. Nevertheless, both the selection of targets and the research itself will have to be conducted within a comprehensive analytical framework.

Because most people are ignorant about most things, it is necessary to look for the kinds of ignorance that cause the most damage and therefore will result in the most benefit when addressed. In other words, research needs to determine who is ignorant about what and where the ignorance is of greatest consequence. In general, there are several kinds of ignorance, and they can be ranked by their potential for negative repercussions.

First, there is ignorance of self. People who have limited knowledge of themselves, their passions, and their goals are doomed to struggle, whether as workers, managers, spouses, parents, or friends.

When it comes to those members of the computing industry who believe that the above observations are either fluff or wholly inapplicable to the world of digital exchange, there is reason to both fear for their souls and expect that the next great developments in computing will pass them by. And if they cannot see the connection between software and self-knowledge, then the problem is their imagination, not their analysis. (If you have just thought of a great software product for this application, you probably have not. The matter is too complex for spur-of-the-moment inspiration.)

Second, there is the ignorance of process: the process of successful accomplishment of any kind, the process of learning, the process of the scientific method and intellectual inquiry, the process of the marketplace, and any other processes that are appropriate to specific activities. And each one of the above processes is listed in order of its consequences. To be ignorant of the process of accomplishment is to virtually guarantee you cannot achieve significant success. And in high-risk situations, you become a menace to public safety and financial solvency. Without an understanding of accomplishment, you cannot succeed as a student. Unless you understand the process of being a student, you cannot be a researcher. And to fail as a student and researcher is to guarantee that you will be as dumb as a doorknob. If you lack an understanding of the marketplace, you are likely to starve. And even after these other conditions have been satisfied, you must still gain an understanding of the processes involved in your specific undertaking. These latter processes — that is, our knowledge of how to do and make things — are also called technology.

Third, there is the ignorance of specific information relevant to the task at hand, often called enabling information. Rapid improvements in complex technologies press all of us to stay abreast of a thousand details. The volume of information is already overwhelming, and it is about to get worse. The term "information overload" does not do justice to the explosion of technological information; the challenge might better be described as information breakdown.

Fourth, there is the ignorance of context. This is the failure to understand any fact in terms of its relationships with other information, both direct and indirect, immediate and eventual, strong and peripheral. Understanding context is the equivalent of being able to see a series of concentric rings emanating from a single impulse, intersecting those of a dozen different impulses. Without the knowledge of context, you are ready prey for the law of unintended consequences. You will always be surprised, and you will almost inevitably fail to find commercial opportunities of consequence. As such opportunities grow and evolve, they almost always cross the boundaries of narrow and specific domains. An opportunity is a good idea that appears where you least expect to find it and has a use where you least expect to be able to apply it.

Context is the knowledge that comes from the integration of disparate data, and from the integration of those integrations. It is a committed multidisciplinary approach. It is *multi*disciplinary, not interdisciplinary or cross-disciplinary. And that means it is an approach that engages a broad bundle of disciplines, without which one cannot even taste the experiences of humanity. Of course, this approach is very difficult, given how hard it is to master even a single discipline of thought. But that is exactly the point, and we wait for computing's expert systems to make it easier. While such a system would have many interconnected elements, several of its features would be clear. For example, it would have a search engine carefully designed to allow the user to search *with ease* for a specified idea across many different kinds of sources (both on the Web and not). (Most of today's engines do not even reliably search all the sites on the Web, and on-line searches of the scholarly databases are at best laborious.) The expert system would then use its rules to hunt down "threads" of relationship among different pieces of information from different sources, in effect creating a story-line. In addition, it would express these often complex threads (or relationships) in a visual form, using colour and geometric structure to highlight areas for further investigation. Each of the above avenues already has product offerings, albeit ones somewhat limited in capability and often operating in isolation from each other. For example, a variety of complex statistical relationships can now be expressed in the multi-coloured simulation of a topographical map.

Fifth, there is the ignorance of the past, the failure to see continuity. Without a knowledge of continuity, it is impossible to understand any interesting (that is, complex) event or circumstance. Unless you know how something came to be, you cannot truly be said to know it. More-over, as the world grows more complex and changes more quickly, there is a need to anticipate ever more dependably future events. But the past is the only raw material out of which to fashion a vision of the future. And the further forward you wish to look, the further back you must go. It is only the truly arrogant who believe that they can violate this rule. (There are those who do violate this rule and do not think of themselves as particularly arrogant; of course, these people believe that historical knowledge is unnecessary because of some reason they expect will occur to them.)

If you wish to observe how unprepared computing is for the future, you should ask any randomly selected member of the industry to provide a condensed history of computing. A few can. Some do no more than cite a few historical facts in no particular order. Some (exhibiting ignorance of, if not disdain for, the social, economic, and business aspects of the industry) actually believe the history of computing comes down to no more than processing speed and the succession of languages.

Interestingly enough, their knowledge of the history of the technology, even narrowly defined, is often shaky. Sometimes it is just wrong. Of course, only a few members of this industry have ever been taught the history of computing, and they live in an industry and a society that do not value this information.

Unfortunately, context and continuity inevitably pull you further and further into the fabric of human society, each thread of causation seemingly without end. But you are driven there as rising competition, together with advancing technology, continues to ratchet up the standard of performance. This standard of performance in turn demands more knowledgeability. The only way to be more capable than someone else is to know more than that person does.

FALSE TRAILS

Awkwardly enough, the marketplace is most in need of context and continuity. Most significant commercial problems (the ones for which competitive advantage pays great rewards) are not restricted to a narrow university- or industry-defined domain. To be successful, you need knowledge about technology, markets, finance, distribution, promotion, psychology, government, and so on. And you need more knowledge about each of these areas today than you did yesterday. It is worth remembering that the marketplace does not care about conventional definitions of specialization; the marketplace, and nothing else, defines relevance. And it is defining this relevance with increasing breadth. It is neither fair nor easy, but the marketplace does not care.

Greater technical specialization, today's most common response to the above challenges, is itself both a self-limiting and a self-defeating process. As the fund of knowledge continues its relentless expansion, an even narrower focus appears necessary. Thus one heart specialist knows only how to treat irregular heartbeats but not how to repair valve damage; a marketing consultant understands only Web-based promotion; a computer scientist knows only how to deploy neural networks. And tomorrow, the specialization will shrink yet again. The heart specialist will address only the heartbeat irregularities of children, the marketing consultant only Web tools for retail, and the scientist only neural networks to target intercontinental ballistic missiles. And we all end up dancing on the head of a pin.

Unfortunately, this process rips apart the context and continuity of knowledge, imperils meaning, and obscures the truth. The answers to complex problems by definition cross boundaries — even while specialization creates them. That stark dilemma must be resolved.

The alternative is to know a lot about a lot. But that was an adequate response for effective problem solving only in the nineteenth century. By the middle of the twentieth century, this approach was basically obsolete. There was already too much knowledge for the generalist to absorb, quite apart from the detailed knowledge that was an essential part of solving the problems at hand. The natural result was to pursue specialization at the cost of less and less general (that is to say, connected) knowledge.

THE BRIGHT SIDE OF THE FORCE

When there is both too much general knowledge and too much detailed knowledge for a person to *know*, the logical response is to enable the person to *command* knowledge instead of knowing it. In other words, we need to make it possible for people to use knowledge they do not have in their heads but do have in their computers. That is exactly what expert systems do. Properly constituted, they provide both breadth and depth of knowledge. That is an ambitious goal, but not an impossible one.

For example, tomorrow's physicians will have to adopt new strategies that include expert systems; if they don't, specializations will become so narrow as to be unworkable. In a hyper-specialized world, a patient with a serious illness would need dozens of physicians. That is more physicians than the world could educate or afford. Instead, most physicians will become organizers of health care. Expert programs will aid in the diagnosis of undetermined illnesses, and much of today's specialist knowledge will be automatically applied to the patient's specific situation. Treatment options will be recommended as well. For most physicians, their principal skill will be the delivery and orchestration of health care in concert with expert systems. While exceptional cases will still go to the specialist physician, the role of the expert system will be to make sure that *only* the exceptional cases are referred on. As is true generally of expert systems, they will absorb the routine (whether complex or not) and leave the anomalies to the human worker.

Even though each area of ignorance has its own particular priority and characteristics, all of them are also fundamentally affected by the absence of benchmarking procedures. It is impossible to describe the nature and importance of a particular kind of ignorance without applying a quantitative measurement. Therefore, it is equally impossible to create an expert system to improve the situation. Of course, it is not a matter of just measuring whether a single person has a particular gap in his or her information set. Rather, if you are a software developer or a consultant, you are trying to measure what is *generally* missing from within a discipline, domain, organization, or industry. The process is basically no more complicated than methodically asking someone questions and noting when they do not know the answers.

There is also the matter of deciding who the ignorant person or agency is. This is not easy. Logic says that the first priority would be to target chief executives of organizations that have the widest economic impact. The ignorance of these people, of course, produces the greatest potential for chaos or pervasive disadvantage. However, it's probably true that many of those who have achieved senior positions are unlikely to appreciate their own ignorance. And it is even less likely for them to see a piece of software as a solution to their deficiency. But if you overcome that obstacle, it is easy to imagine their willingness and ability to pay — and pay handsomely.

More broadly speaking, the urgency of addressing a person's ignorance is in direct relation to that person's decision-making power (the types of decisions made, the organizational level at which they are made, and the size or position of the organization). This may produce some surprising areas of priority. Is it more important to address the ignorance of the director of R&D or that of the vice-president of finance? The manager of human resources or the head of purchasing? In company X or Y? In industry A or B?

It might be argued that this precision is unnecessary, that there is a generic software system that would address all these instances of ignorance with equal effectiveness. And there is a possibility that at least a family of solutions would serve. But you could not know whether a single approach would satisfy the needs of disparate users unless you first understood exactly what those needs were.

The scale of the consequences of ignorance is also a function of the number of people involved, apart from other considerations. Ignorance that affects a million people is more dangerous than ignorance affecting a thousand. Here, in the mass market of ignorance, the key issue would then be to decide which of the thousands of possible pieces of omitted information has the greatest impact. Again, the answer will not immediately be obvious.

Fortunately, people do exhibit similarities based on some shared characteristics. Those with similar educational backgrounds tend to display similar areas of ignorance. Indeed, some blind spots are notoriously easy to predict. Certain industries and occupations also invite their own peculiarities of ignorance. And the culture of companies can do so as well. Age and other socio-economic characteristics also appear to have some effect. Engineers are often uncomfortable with behavioural concerns, for example, and lawyers with business priorities. Mathematicians tend to lack verbal skills and historians lack quantitative ones. Automotive executives hate radical changes and software executives want killer applications. The pharmaceutical industry understands long-term research and the entertainment industry sees no need for it. The young tend to have little time for historical information and the old resist the latest developments. All of us struggle with the limitations of our own perspective. But nothing is so clear that it can be assumed without careful consideration.

While the process of documenting and understanding knowledge and its companion, ignorance, is a time-consuming and expensive one, it is by no means impossible. And the very scope of ignorance makes it likely that useful observations will result. Yet because of limits on the technology of artificial intelligence, those in the computing industry insist on believing that expert systems are speculative possibilities; they do not notice that the limit is really our unwillingness to explore the problem of ignorance. Even scholarly commentators on expert systems stress the importance of documenting what experts know, instead of what users do not know.

The foregoing discussion about ignorance is no more than a barebones argument. Although the absence of benchmarking procedures has attracted little applied research, there is a vast literature concerning the philosophy and taxonomy of knowledge. Nevertheless, a full exploration of these issues has hardly begun. The mastery of these complex debates is, of course, essential to the fundamental thrust of computing.

The response to these information deficiencies has been limited because of unwarranted assumptions. First, it is taken for granted that since you cannot know everything, you must delegate that function to others; this is the most common response of senior executives. They expect to respond to their ignorance with briefings by their seconds-in-command, who overcome their own ignorance by being briefed by their subordinates. But are any of these people actually drawing on their own knowledge? Or are they doing ad hoc research to fill an order for information quickly? Even if delegation was an adequate response to ignorance, in most organizations this "briefing" function is merely tacked on to an already overloaded job description. Or it is delegated to a junior who has no one left to push it to. Or it is delegated to an in-house researcher who is overburdened (or would be if all the relevant ignorance was being addressed).

The real problem is the ad hoc quality of these delegations. By their very nature, they fail to provide either context or continuity. And while most companies expect someone to be providing a watching brief, it is often done casually, without a particular profile or resources. Of course, when companies need a large dose of information, they call in the experts, the consultants. Sometimes these consultants do provide important expertise and information, and they often offer the value of an outsider's objective opinion. But at other times, the consultants, who are the children of their culture, exhibit their own ignorance.

Let's consider the executive who is questioned about his command of information and points to the company's exhaustive financial reports: cash flows, budgets, balance sheets, income statements, and cost-benefit analyses. While that is a good start, the executive often has little else to show, which betrays an ignorance of context and continuity, at the very least. Financial information, vital though it is (and amazingly absent as it sometimes is), is not a summary of all reality, even in the domain of business. To act as if it is, even implicitly, is to invite accountants to recreate Frankenstein's monster. The state of knowledge, as a topic in its own right, is so undeveloped that we do not know, and have barely studied, the degree to which financial values can capture broad economic realities.

The scope of the ignorance discussed above and the care that must be taken to understand it are the reasons that so much commercial advantage awaits. First, since the problem of ignorance is largely unrecognized, and since it cannot be easily or quickly understood, there are relatively few competitors in the expert-system marketplace today, and even fewer who are trying to advance to the next level of sophistication. Second, precisely because the ignorance is so pervasive, it takes but a small improvement in knowledge to produce a major impact. After all, a single candle in a cave of riches should easily lead to treasure.

Consider the entertainment industry, an endeavour where intellectual prowess is not always readily apparent. The industry is notoriously volatile, driven as it is by blockbuster hits or outright disasters. Its participants take as an article of faith that it is impossible to reliably predict which movie will score big. At the same time, they (and their customers) complain that too many offerings are imitative and boring. Where, ask the studio executives, are the new ideas? Old ideas can be recycled only so often before the customer tunes out and decides to play golf instead.

An examination of the entertainment industry will also reveal that many of its participants are ignorant (as a descriptive word) of the world's literature, of literary scholarship, of history as a source of stories, and of storytelling as an art. In the face of such ignorance, of course, ideas are simply duplicated again and again. The opening for a series of expert systems is wide indeed. We await an expert system that stores the characteristics of all the world's great stories, codified as good story rules. Some are for plot, others for character. Some are for timing, some for imagery. There can be expert systems that have stored, in an organized form, the history of movies, with rules deduced by the pattern-recognition software already in existence.

The first of these systems will not work perfectly; it may not even work well. But given the randomness of the performance of this particular industry, a 20 percent improvement would translate into much new profit. With the precedent set and the resources available, the expert systems could then grow in their reliability.

When Edgar Bronfman, as the new head of Universal, tried to impose a more business-like approach to moviemaking, his critics in Hollywood laughed in derision. But all he needed were the tools.

VISION OR MISSION?

The great rebuttal to any assertion that ignorance is dangerously rampant is the observation that while we do not live in paradise, the economy is growing steadily (as it usually does) and technology continues to move forward. This sense of complacency, together with an assumption of the inevitability of ignorance, is the essential barrier to the progress of knowledge. But the advancing economy is irrelevant to this argument, and to presume otherwise is to exhibit ignorance of one of the central principles of economics: opportunity cost. This principle holds that the ideal decision is the one that produces the highest possible benefit, not just *some* benefit. The principle is overlooked in many circumstances, but it is overlooked with the greatest damage with respect to knowledgeability. The point is not to trumpet what we have accomplished in our present state of ignorance, but to imagine what we could accomplish in a diminished state of ignorance.

There is an alternative to our present course of taking pot shots at ignorance. This alternative would increase the revenues and profits of the computing industry, speed the pace of the economy, accelerate the growth in the standard of living, lower the death rate, and enhance environmental protection, among other things. The benefits we forego by not taking a new approach to knowledgeability are incalculable. The essential difference between those who will take computing to its next level and those who will not is their understanding of human capability. Some believe that interconnecting the world will alone cause a quantum leap forward in society's productivity and happiness. This view treats humans as machines for information consumption; if you provide, they will eat. There are others who have no interest in human capability or its improvement. They see computing as just another product to sell to the mindless masses, a bedazzling pastime for consumers as they wait for death.

But there are those who understand intimately the great gap between the current state of humanity and its potential. They intend to wage war on ignorance using all their resources, showing no mercy and taking no prisoners. They believe that with the right product, they will reap an overwhelming response. They know computing tools are not all that is required to fully vanquish ignorance, but they see them as indispensable.

CHAPTER SIX

FOUNDATION OF EMPIRE

GUARANTEED MONOPOLY

Expert systems are about power: who has it, who needs it, and who will pay for it. These power relationships are the essential characteristics of high-level expert systems, and this is what gives them relevance beyond a narrow niche market. Expert systems are more than general business applications renamed. Since they help businesses make more effective decisions about critical problems from marketing to personnel to finance, they can create powerful competitive advantages. Expert systems are moving beyond such useful functions as tightening the supply chain to the prevention of mistakes and the discovery of opportunity. The company that has the software to deliver these functions is obviously in a strong bargaining position; it will easily be able to command a premium profit margin. Moreover, given the money and power involved, it is not difficult to image that some deep-pocketed customers will pay for exclusive rights to certain expert systems — so that they can have a proprietary way to increase their profits faster than their competitors.

However, some may doubt whether the developer of the expert system will actually have the ability to extract rich profits. Conventional wisdom says no. The massive potential for profit from expert systems will cause other developers to rush out products that mimic any that prove to be successful (except in the narrowest of applications). The second or third movers may even have such superior market skills and resources that they can use to relegate the pioneer to secondary status. Netscape was first with browsers but found itself yielding to Microsoft's Explorer. However, that possibility is irrelevant for most fully developed expert systems. The conventional view assumes, often without even explicitly saying so, that the barriers to entry for software are weak. This is especially the case, many claim, since the state-sanctioned monopolies that arise through intellectual property (IP) rights such as patents and copyrights often do not offer much effective protection.

But this conventional view is wrong. While standard software is often very difficult to protect as intellectual property, expert systems are very different from the software that exists today. These differences make them protectable, even easily protectable. Very valuable + easily protected = a recipe for monopoly status and monopoly profits.

Since the full commercial potential of expert systems is itself unrecognized, it is not surprising that little attention has been devoted to their IP rights. The fact that these rights are often assumed to be straightforward and simple is part of the problem. The issues surrounding IP rights are underappreciated by both the law and the information industries.

The law has spent most of its centuries of evolution ignoring information as property because there was no demand or need for it to do otherwise. Even as copyrights and patents came into use, they applied to only a relatively narrow slice of economic activity. And the infrequent litigation that did happen tended to focus on relatively narrow points. That has now changed.

As has long been the case, a patent is granted only for an application that is new — an advance in the state of the art, in other words — not for an obvious evolution or iteration of an existing technology (together with other qualifying characteristics). For example, an office chair with an extra wheel would be unpatentable (even if it worked better) because it would be considered an "obvious" improvement in chair technology. By contrast, an office chair that was guaranteed never to tip over might be patentable if the anti-tipping mechanism had never been available before. Of course, there is an element of subjectivity when it comes to deciding what is obvious and what is not, and in the final analysis, these issues are decided in court. Copyright, another major form of IP, is meant to protect literary and artistic works from unauthorized reproduction. Software has used both patent and copyright protections with varying degrees of success.

The range of legal protections has been strengthened by both practice and legislation, and IP is a growing legal specialty. In an economy where innovation is your only safe route to competitive advantage, the legal rights to that innovation become critically important. And rising competition only strengthens the need to retain these rights. Of course, this observation is commonplace. What is odd is how little actual response from developers occurs (although it should be observed that in this, as in other matters, talk without action is truly commonplace).

It is true that in those parts of the information industry where IP protection has a long-standing history and is essential for success, these legal protections are quite well developed. The movie and music industries are examples, although here technology is overriding the law and unpunished piracy continues to thrive.

The problem, it must be emphasized, is not an utter lack of response to IP issues; it is that the response is not commensurate with the potential commercial benefits. However, because this is a problem of degree, and because it is difficult to show degree, most players continue to congratulate themselves on their IP strategies.

FREE SOFTWARE?

Nowhere in the information industry is the tentative state of our understanding more apparent than in the domain of proprietary software. Key assumptions are eroding under the pressures of the changing marketplace, and what was once true is now proving to be either incomplete or incorrect. Consider, for example, the software industry's common assumption that copyright protection is basically a legal issue, although competent lawyers know that it is not. Developers tend to create a product and then ship it off to their legal advisers to see if it can be protected. If it cannot, then the developer's strategy is to run like the wind, getting the product on the market as quickly as possible. This is partly the result of a widespread belief that, in most cases, software is inherently unprotectable, even while everyone involved pretends that it is not. The only protectable software is assumed to be that with specific niche applications.

This belief arises from the view that most software development is merely a matter of programming time and resources, and that it does not involve unique intellectual insight. In other words, most people believe that any software-related problem can be solved with only modest effort; they don't imagine it takes any real creativity. And there's no question that a lot of software is imitative, and that imitating the designs of others isn't usually difficult. Even if the exact steps to a software solution have been protected, one need only find different steps to the same result. And given the cheapness of power and memory, it often does not matter whether an application uses twelve or twenty-two steps. It is therefore not surprising that in such circumstances, legal protections are seen by most participants as little more than delaying tactics or smokescreens. In a legal sense, most software is either an imitation or an evolutionary iteration, the next obvious step in a well-understood continuing process. But what is even more apparent is the intellectual quandary into which the industry is falling.

In the early days of software development, most computing tasks were straightforward and had obvious, unprotectable answers. These were well-understood tasks that needed to be computerized (like spreadsheets), and there was no doubt about what had to be created. But with expert systems, the answers are not obvious or simple. These more mature tasks cannot simply be described as difficult or complex, however, because it is a characteristic of computing that even obvious steps involve complex programming. The complexity of the programming is, by itself, not usually sufficient to create a strongly protected product.

And this is why the discussion can become confused. Developers and their lawyers do not always distinguish between the complexity of the solution and the complexity of the software that executes the solution. The solution can be obvious (and therefore unpatentable), even while the execution of that solution is complex and non-obvious. Or it could be the other way around, with the solution complex and the software routine. And of course, complexity alone does not necessarily create patent protectability, since it could be interpreted as no more than a long series of obvious steps. Even the law itself is not wholly clear on the issue of when complexity renders a solution non-obvious.

RESEARCH RULES

However, as expert systems tackle complex problems that go beyond the codification of rules, they begin to deliver characteristics that positively invite strong IP protection. These systems use rules that are the result of genuine research. This proprietary knowledge is then expressed as a complex set of interrelated rules. The system itself will have explicitly searched for and validated the relevant rules, crossing multidisciplinary boundaries. In other words, the expert system will often appear as a highly complex and therefore non-obvious solution. It will, in a fundamental sense, appear as either an intricate "mechanical" device or a content-intensive "novel."

For example, the developer of an expert system to improve moviemaking will presumably use multidisciplinary research to create a set of rules that will increase the odds of generating a commercially successful product. The rules are likely to be very complex (after all, if it was easy to create blockbusters, it would happen much more frequently).

The complexity would arise from both the number and detail of the rules and their precise sequencing. The system would not, for instance, have a rule that would recommend using "interesting" characters; it would instead suggest forty-two specific ways to create dependably interesting characters. There would be equally detailed rules for all the other elements of a story, from plot to setting. In effect, such an expert system would consist of a long series of "non-obvious" steps (because the obvious ways to make movies do not work very well).

If we assume that the system works well enough to make it profitable (which it must do for its IP protections to be relevant), then the more non-obvious aspects it has, the more protectable it becomes. And if this non-obvious content arose from private research, the courts will tend to uphold proprietary rights. In any event, the longer and more detailed the rules, the more copyright applies. And because expert systems offer detailed solutions in precise sequences, and their effectiveness is buried in the details, competitors cannot simply juggle the content to escape copyright or patent protections.

Of course, feasible solutions produced by intensive research do not alone qualify for legal protection. But if the software developers are not attempting to solve a research-dependent task, they are not even within the pool from which a subset of protectable solutions is drawn. And as we have noted, the software industry as a whole does relatively little research. Therefore, the key determinant of legal protection is largely absent, and thus there are relatively few products with strong legal protections.

Nevertheless, almost all software products stake out legal protection of one kind or another. However, many of these legal claims are either untested or ignored. Products that dominate their markets usually do so as the result of their marketing strength or strategy, and not as the result of a legal monopoly. Unfortunately, any discussion of research-dependent expert systems is often clouded by the industry's assumption that this necessarily means the field of artificial intelligence (AI).

There is a middle ground, however, between insignificant software and AI — a place where the research is genuine, where the results offer commercial advantage, where the odds of success are reasonable and remain on this side of epic breakthrough. In other words, it is possible to push conventional programming technology into non-obvious research without transforming the technology itself. Existing expert systems are proof enough of this, since with today's software technology they work effectively in applications ranging from medicine to industrial design. The preceding examples in message management and entertainment also need draw on no more than the standard techniques. Nevertheless, many important business problems that invite expert systems are left unaddressed because developers *assume*, having conducted no research, that such a system is impossible without an advance in software technology. And yet, for any particular problem, this middle way cannot be said to be impossible until it has been tried many times. Conventional software can have unconventional applications, if only it is asked to do so.

CONTENT IS KING

This challenge is so seldom undertaken because developers fail to see both what is needed and how research could answer that need. This failure is not surprising in an industry that serves the most intimate and subtle of human purposes with a focus that is normally narrow in the extreme. In many cases, there is no context whatsoever for the software product. Not only is the product not positioned within the overall software market, but it is also not placed within the context of computing or the broader information industry.

However, since information has reality only within the human mind, it is impossible to truly fathom its uses, except in a multidisciplinary context that bridges the scope of society with the dictates of machinery. Until the software industry accepts and acts on this logic, we remain in the early and chaotic days of the information age. It should be emphasized that a multidisciplinary approach should be used at every stage of product development. Legal advisers, for example, are often brought into the process far too late, and market analysis is also seen as a separate and later issue. Yet only when all the relevant disciplines are integrated do a product's serious proprietary implications become apparent.

For example, a business task may appear to have an obvious, non-protectable answer when it's viewed in a one-dimensional space. However, when the task is revisited in a multidisciplinary context, it often becomes clear that the first answer was either incorrect or incomplete, and that the problem does not really have an obvious or known solution. The hospitality industry, for instance, knows perfectly well that front-line staff must deliver "friendly" service in order to have satisfied and, more important, repeat customers. The obvious way to achieve this is to hire people with naturally friendly personalities and to reinforce this attitude with "friendliness" training and appropriate recognition. Unfortunately, even though the above technique is commonly applied, *consistently* friendly service remains notoriously difficult to deliver. Different organizations apply this same basic approach but produce very different degrees of service. Thus Disney sets a very high standard of friendly service on a consistent basis, while certain hotel chains, using similar approaches, do not. It becomes clear that the obvious answer is flawed, and that the real answer lies in the details of what Disney does that others do not. In other words, there are missing elements — other dimensions — that must be considered. The real answer is more complicated than the obvious one. And the real answer asks for more thought and research. Exactly what is Disney doing that makes its service exceptional? What key steps are others omitting or forgetting?

Of course, this broader context offers guidance in the search for proprietary technology. For example, we know software is content and content is protectable. To see software as separate from content, as only the manipulation of content, is fundamentally incorrect. In fact, it is hard to see how software could even be defined as separate from content. But then the central question becomes why is content protection (that is, copyright) relatively ineffective for software when it provides a powerful monopoly to a company like Disney? This is especially confusing given that Disney can protect content as inconsequential as the image of a rodent.

The problem for expert software may not be that content protection is inapplicable, but that there is not enough content (or enough of the right content) to make it protectable. But where would more content for an instruction set come from? If the software problem — that is, the business problem that the system was meant to address — had no single or easy answer, then the research that eventually provided the answer could be embedded in the software. In other words, developers could draw on their research to produce content-intensive software. But content-intensive software is not an expert system that just has 2,000 logically obvious steps as opposed to 500. It is "calibrated" software that contains information that was discovered in the research, and that if not reproduced exactly renders the software inoperative. Such information might enjoy copyright protection and serve as a strong barrier to imitation, since "close" duplication would not work.

There appears to be a variety of information, both numerical and otherwise, that would qualify for calibration. An expert investment adviser would be a case in point. It would naturally base many of its rules on a precise value (e.g., do not invest if a certain measurement is below 0.213). But it could just as easily specify fourteen sources of information whose influence is precisely weighted (e.g., investment information from source number one is twice as important as that from source number two, but half as important as that from source number eight).

Of course, it is also possible that research would result in expert systems that could be patentable and could stand the test of actual litigation. It appears that such "inventive" expert software would grow out of process problems of particular complexity. For example, an expert system designed to discover better drug therapies might be so intricate that its rule sequences appear "ingenious." This is the attribute that patent laws are intended to encourage.

As the computer industry is required to adapt to increasingly intense competition and faster technological change, its responses will have to become progressively more thoughtful at every level. It cannot be any other way for the industry that produces one of the most sophisticated products in the marketplace. This inevitably will result in an integrated multidisciplinary approach from which will evolve entirely new categories of expert software. Unfortunately, for the moment, the software industry is distracted by the demand for its obvious products and the hyperactive financial markets. And of course, none of the above recommendations will be acted on by the wheeler-dealers with which computing is afflicted.

POWER OF MONOPOLY PROFIT

An appropriately aggressive IP strategy will be adopted by most members of the software industry because the marketplace will reward them with extraordinary profit. The only issues are the speed with which this will occur and whether today's dominant players will lead this trend or be devastated by it. There is no particular reason why the established players should not be able to adopt this kind of strategy. They will find it progressively more difficult to sell obvious software solutions at high profit and volume. Older solutions fade in profitability over time, and there are only a few obvious solutions left for exploitation. The "upgrade" tactic is also self-limiting, and for some products, it is already at the limit of what the client will tolerate.

A forward-looking IP strategy starts with the acknowledgement that the next plateau of computing rests on the strong proprietary protections of expert systems. Branding will remain an important marketing tool, but it will not ensure profitability. The search for proprietary advantage must, of course, be tightly integrated with a pursuit of market opportunity. It will be especially important for developers to look beyond obvious solutions; the problem of the client may still be obvious, even though its solution is not.

Research will produce solutions with varying degrees of effectiveness. An excellent solution might involve a complex set of numerical data derived from a rapidly changing situation, where the method used to derive the observations is a trade secret, known only to the developer. In circumstances such as this, copyright could be a very powerful protection. Other companies could not just duplicate the results of the first mover; they would have to take the time to conduct their own research and generate an answer of their own. But by then, the original developer should have advanced further into the problem. This is the advantage of dealing with a complex problem: the possibilities for improvement are not easily exhausted. This creates, in turn, true upgrades, where the user is manifestly better served by each version.

The challenge of such an approach is to persuade clients that the calibrations of the expert system are valid without revealing the research methodology. There are several ways to do this, not the least of which is to have accounting firms "attest" that the calibrations are valid. It should also be possible to persuade the client to buy based purely on the effectiveness of the result. An expert system should, after all, work much better than non-expert software (or the research itself is flawed, in which case that, not marketing, is the problem).

An ideal solution entirely sidesteps the issue of patent and copyright, and relies instead on trade secrets, a tool with thousands of years of tradition behind it. Here the protection lasts as long as the key methodology is kept hidden from competitors. Patents, by contrast, require the holder to tell the world exactly how the patented effect is produced. Of course, the best way to protect a product is not to sell it. This is the model of the application service provider (ASP). These companies maintain software in their own facilities and use the Internet to deliver software functions to their clients. After some initial hype, however, ASPs have settled down to deliver only generic functions with modest results. The problem, as is the case for much of the software industry, is that the ASP usually offers no exceptional or exclusive function.

However, an expert system delivered in the ASP mode would clearly be a profit machine. An expert system that delivered a critical business function (for example, selecting senior managerial talent) would run in its own facility and deliver its advice to the client via the Internet. As the expert system continued its research, it would adjust itself (called "learning" by people who think machines are alive) to improve its performance. A competitor would have to repeat the original effort merely to duplicate the initial form of the expert system. But by then, the first system would already have evolved based on its exclusive experience with its clients. The competitor would be in the unenviable position of having to catch a moving target. And the client would know only that the product works, not *how* it works. Fees for such a system would, of course, be exorbitant, but the option for the client is to choose executives in a demonstrably less effective fashion.

RESCUE THE CARMAKERS

The critic will again announce that software with such effective and valuable functions is beyond the developer's ability to create using contemporary technology. But that merely reminds us that the critic has thought about the problem for a minute instead of for five years. This view assumes that ignorance and flawed decision making is of minor consequence. It assumes that commanding information is a simple matter.

Consider a hypothetical example. An expert system to help market automobiles would be in high demand. The automobile market is very competitive, and several of its key players are struggling. North American producers continue to lose market share to imports, and General Motors has especially struggled. Clearly, their present strategies do not work as well as the car companies would like. There can be little doubt that they would buy a system that delivered superior marketing results. This is, of course, a computing problem.

That many people do not think so is a sign of the immaturity of the computing industry. But automobile marketing is a computing problem because it is, first and foremost, an information problem. Information about what the customer wants and knows must be matched with information about the vehicles available and the conditions under which they are offered. Plainly, there is not enough information currently at hand to help carmakers better serve the needs of their customers. But there are several avenues available to greatly increase the information set — and all involve research. First, using all the information tools already available, the system developer would assemble *all* the relevant scientific information, both digital and non-digital, concerning automobile sales (from consumer surveys to macroeconomic indicators such as interest rates). He or she will also consider any factors that affect similar "big ticket" items, such as major household appliances. This alone is a major task, and one without end (since the underlying flow of information does not stop).

Of course, research like this has already been conducted. But since it has not helped General Motors, the research obviously is not finished and the opportunity remains. Or are we to conclude that since a *piece* of research produced no immediate answers, the answer is impossible to find? Fortunately, cancer researchers don't think this way.

As we discussed, the market opening for expert systems is so wide because we live in a world that does not truly value research, and that does not conduct research aggressively, intensively, or relentlessly enough. That is why there are expert rules (many of which can be made to be proprietary) waiting to be uncovered. In the case of the automotive industry, expert systems will even be needed to both manage and verify the information collected during the research period. For example, screening tools will remove unscientific observations. This verification process is poorly done in many areas of research, including academic research, because it is more convenient for a researcher to assume that someone else has verified a piece of information he or she wishes to use. So the information is "cited" back to its original source, although that describes its pedigree, not its veracity. (Information attributed to a source is of better quality than unattributed information, of course, but only barely.) Because verifying the information is admittedly a lot of work, part of the process must be computerized in an expert system that checks for verification hallmarks. But the task must be undertaken, whether the developer draws on an existing verification system, creates one for the current job, or conducts the process laboriously by hand. Logic says this is likely the way to unearth the golden expert rule.

The material uncovered during the research phase is then assembled into a carefully structured database from which two sets of observations should emerge. First, there will be key characteristics that will show a relationship between automotive sales and various causal factors. Second, the research will highlight gaps that appear to stand in the way of a better understanding of this issue. What the developer finds is not necessarily what is most critically necessary.

An aggressive developer may be tempted to commission his or her own specific research to fill the most critical of these gaps. Generally, research tends to look at the relationship between two variables, such as that between the consumer's income and the model of car purchased, using an observation set of a hundred data points, a minuscule part of the whole equation. And while statistical tools can provide representativeness, there is always a need for more evidence. What is enough data for one class of discoveries may be wholly inadequate for a different class. And often the absence of evidence is offered as the proof of the absence of a causal connection — a typical error in an ignorant society. In this situation, the developer, as information researcher, looks for ways to find more evidence to prove that causal connection.

An equally important research initiative would document the ignorance of those responsible for marketing cars (this would include errors communicated by marketing to design). This is an attempt to determine whether automotive executives make assumptions that are inconsistent with the information that has already been collected. For example, they could assume that gas mileage is modestly relevant to the customer, when in fact it is critically important. Since this research requires the screening of large amounts of data, it is a perfect computer task. (A couple of focus groups involving auto executives is a starting point for this research, not a substitute for it.) Also, since the developer would have no way of knowing where the error is, he or she would need to document the ignorance of the automotive sales force, as well as that of the customers. This ignorance profile will almost certainly detect serious errors. There will be strong relationships that are unknown, denied, or ignored. There will be alleged relationships that have been emphatically disproved. This is not an insult to the automotive industry, however. Unless this industry turns out to be a calm oasis peopled by enlightened truth-seekers in a largely ignorant world, it is likely to be somewhat confused, like the rest of the world. Battling this confusion is what the expert system is intended to do.

At this stage, the expert developers may have the insight they need to offer their services; if not, they keep working until they do. The ultimate solution is a rule, validated by research, about how to sell more cars; the rule is likely to be very complicated (i.e., content-rich), *and* it is either unknown to members of the industry or known but not acted upon.

The automotive industry's typically large companies invite information disorder. Complete information may not always be communicated to the right players at the right time. Perhaps the research will "prove" what has long been suspected: that the lack of co-ordination between marketing and design is the real reason some cars are hard to sell. Misinformation will likely persist, of course, and some information will not be acted upon. But a properly implemented expert system can address any of these issues.

Thus the developer who undertakes this considerable research effort will be able to turn a proprietary understanding of the marketing of automobiles into a unique and advanced guide to improved sales.

THE SOLUTION

In some situations, this will also be an important consulting opportunity. However, the full solution will be manifestly a piece of software. It is likely to be too information-intensive to be delivered efficiently except in the form of software. That was, after all, the point of the exercise: to use information aggressively to solve a management problem. This hypothetical solution might have identified, say, 112 key marketing tasks associated with increased sales success, and for each of these there might be nineteen sub-tasks. Perhaps this has been done for five categories of vehicles, producing thousands of marketing configurations. This is a strategy for marketing and promotion that is, as a practical matter, impossible without a computer, exactly the kind of task that a developer seeks.

The resulting piece of software will recognize the depth and complexity of human motivations and needs, rejecting the simplistic and unproven notion that a ten-item checklist is all you need to evaluate an automobile or a sales campaign. It rejects vague decision-makers who make choices based on gut instinct or experience. It challenges everyone to use logic and evidence to address this critical function, and demands that they generate the information without which it is foolhardy to proceed. And it will chide the careless.

Some will counter that there are intangible aspects of human behaviour that cannot be measured. This anti-intellectual assertion has little place in the information industries. Of course, some aspects of behaviour will be immune to measurement, but that observation only *limits* the effectiveness of the solution. (If this limitation guts the effectiveness of the solution, the research continues.) And in light of how poorly information is presently used and organized, the odds of a better solution proceeding from better (but not perfect) information are high. The goal is not an impossibly perfect result. The design for the present version of Ford's F-series trucks, for example, almost went ahead without a rigorous investigation of consumer preference. Fortunately, a determined internal advocate insisted on a greater degree of research. The result was a different design and stronger sales. Still, no one would claim that this was a perfect truck design, or that Ford won over every single customer it might have. Yet sales were better than they would have been.

Therefore, Version 1.0 of Auto Marketing will have omitted some characteristics, either because they required more research or because they resisted measurement. All that means is that the research process continues; what was unmeasurable today may be measurable tomorrow. This is the process of science. And tomorrow's evidence may indeed contradict today's, which is why the latest findings will have to be integrated into the program and its internal values recalibrated. The expert system will never be finished.

In addition, the IP protections for this kind of software should be powerful. The program will contain a large amount of unique information generated by the developer using trade-secret procedures. Since this information should attract copyright, if nothing else, it cannot simply be duplicated by a competitor. Some results could be duplicated from information in the public domain, but that would first require the imitator to develop a research tool to uncover that information. That and the fact that the research period itself is lengthy constitute a strong barrier to entry. Of course, the original developer also continues the research, keeping ahead of any imitator that does emerge. Still, it must be admitted that no barrier to entry is forever assured.

Even with copyright protection, keeping the research procedure secret will be a high priority. The problem then is how to persuade the client that the system's rules actually produce improved results. The answer is quite simple: offer a pilot to prove its effectiveness. Or offer payment only on performance. This, of course, requires the developers to trust both science and their own competence. But that is no more than high-level enterprise.

Interestingly enough, there are those who grant that such expert systems could constitute a profitable "niche" market, but they fail to see its scale compared to the mass market that exists for business software. There are two responses to this concern. First, we must realize that the auto industry earns many billions of dollars in profits, and that this expert system will expect performance pay. If the system were to increase sales by $500 million, a fair share of that would be demanded by the developer. Depending on the success of the system, the reward to the developer will range from handsome to breathtaking. The point is not how many customers you have, it is how much profit you make. This obvious distinction still seems to confuse the software industry.

In addition, there are the marketing systems for the major assemblers, for the auto parts suppliers, and for the dealers themselves. Each has specific needs, although each can still be efficiently driven off the same research base. Moreover, there is an opportunity to develop an elite, and very expensive, version of the expert system for each major manufacturer, a version that is suited to their particular circumstances, and that they can customize on an ongoing basis to give the possibility of a unique competitive advantage.

Second, after the automobile market has been fully serviced and is providing an indefinite stream of licensing fees, the developer will decide how much of its basic methodology could be transferred to an allied market. There may well be other products or services that have car-like marketing characteristics. Mutual funds, for example? There would still be a need for considerable research concerning the specifics of a new market, of course, but now the developer would be able to build on established platforms and procedures.

BATTLE ROYAL

There are a large number of complex problems that appear suited to expert systems, and to which the above research-and-protection procedure would apply. They can be found in most businesses and in not-for-profit organizations from schools to hospitals. Each of these problems would have a similar distinguishing characteristic: there is a vast amount of data that cannot be interpreted without the assistance of computing. However, much of the business world, including computing, assumes that software's only role is to organize and sort (i.e., search) large databases. Database management is of course necessary, but it is only a part of the interpretive task. Indeed, database-management tools are still not used in as many applications and as aggressively as they could be. This is partly because the database software has limitations that need to be corrected and partly because some uses are apparent only when the developer is trying to truly interpret information.

The main obstacle to expert systems is the assumption that software can do no more than manipulate these vast stores of data. But what software must really do is express the data within the instruction set — that is, it must express the essential elements or characteristics of the relevant data. Software must become one with content, showing both the strengths and the deficiencies of the existing information base. Until this happens, we can neither make effective use of the information we have nor find the information we need to generate.

And since the mirror has trouble looking at itself, it needs to be observed that this approach applies to the computing industry, as well as to almost all other users. So, for example, software to "mine" data should be built on a thorough understanding of all the ways data and databases can be organized. Some programmers think they have done this; they have the odd idea that the organization of human knowledge is a small problem to be addressed in a few days of client consultations. Actually, this problem has tormented philosophers and librarians for centuries, and its resolution requires thousands of hours of research and analysis. To think otherwise is to exhibit a degree of either ignorance or arrogance that would be stunning for any member of the information industry. This is not to deny that "mining" software in its primitive form addresses some obvious needs, or that useful guidance can result from this software. But this is merely the opening shot for a product of critical importance. Presumably, the developers who are specializing in this area, and those who wish to, are already at work on the research that will make the market.

In a world of fierce competitive struggle, the expert system's ability to bestow competitive advantage is power indeed. And a monopoly supplier of such an advantage would possess power sublime. With so much money and power at risk, many of the major players will be tempted to engage in heroic and bloody battle.

Most of those already in the computer industry, from the largest of the software providers to the smallest and the newest, will find themselves in this competitive arena. They will seek the holy grail of monopoly while at the same time trying to break down the monopolies of their competitors. And the clients will be in the thick of it. Large and powerful organizations will not enjoy buying their software from monopoly sources; they will surely fear that their core competency is in the hands of third parties. Thus many clients will feel they have no choice but to join the battle directly, taking on the development of their expert systems themselves. Indeed, depending on the fierceness of the struggle, much of computer development will potentially be sucked back into the customer's fold. While takeovers of software firms by non-software firms are uncommon today, they will be inevitable in the future, given the need for competitive advantage. That will merely set off another wave of computer consolidation as software developers try to defend themselves against their clients, rather than each other.

In the middle of this struggle there may well emerge an entirely new type of software developer; these people will call themselves software creators and will specialize in using computers to create meaning. They will try to operate with a level of skill, experience, and sophistication that their clients will be unable to match. They will be the ones to develop the most elite of the expert systems, the ones that leave no aspect of society untouched.

CHAPTER SEVEN

ADVANCE OF THE SYSTEMS

THE DESTRUCTION THAT AWAITS

Because expert systems will displace human workers, reorganize work flow, challenge every aspect of business, and further accelerate the pace of technological change, great resistance to their adoption can be expected. While the slow and piecemeal advance of the systems has not yet occasioned objection, their gathering force undoubtedly will. But since we do not use most of what we know (and often act on information that is incorrect), and since expert systems mobilize accurate information, there can be no doubt that these systems provide more effective responses. They lower costs, shorten reaction time, and open previously inaccessible avenues for improvement. The waste from management errors and omissions is reduced, as is that from unnecessary communication.

With ignorance so pervasive and competitive pressures so intense, established practice will inevitably yield to the superiority of these systems. Thus management practice will be radically changed, as will education and training. The consulting industry, not surprisingly a keystone in the constellation of IT industries, will also be profoundly affected. Since expert systems can encourage innovation, they will accelerate the number of creative responses hitting the marketplace. The result will be a sharp competitive advantage for those who adopt the systems quickly and aggressively, especially in the beginning, when others are lagging behind. But in the speeding economy of the twenty-first century, when the playing field tilts, there will be a stampede of response.

There should be no doubt that the widespread use of expert systems will severely stress normal business practice. Expert systems inevitably replace part of human work; in many cases, they will, in effect, replace a worker. Eliminating workers is already common practice within the manufacturing industries. But distribution workers are equally at risk, as are clerks of all types. This does not mean that human work is disappearing, but this work is certainly changing in its fundamental nature. The uncertainty alone will cause many people to feel highly threatened. And many workers and managers, it can be assumed, will actively discourage the wide adoption of these systems. Countering this reaction will not be as simple as having senior managers order these changes to be implemented. After all, as soon as expert systems do become widely accepted, they will march their way up the management hierarchy. Thus senior managers will tend to be uneasy about setting off a process for others that will inevitably involve them. Asking the manager of inventory control to defer to an expert program is only a few steps removed from telling the vice-president of marketing that his advertising strategy must be vetted by a similar system.

Every conceivable objection to expert systems will tumble out. While it will be granted that these systems work in a few narrow applications, like industrial process control, they will be pronounced incapable of applying to most other broader areas. It will be claimed that most major business decisions must take into account too many factors with too many subtle attributes ever to be captured by routine programming. Therefore, the argument goes, a management tool can computerize the relationship between buyer and seller, for example, by suggesting an upgraded purchase combination, but it will be unable to deal with the intricate challenges of a new product announcement by a major competitor. While process-control software can respond to changing pressure in a feedstock line, it cannot tell you that half the technology in the plant is now obsolete and needs to be replaced. Expert systems may be able to sort by keywords through a mountain of resumés, but they will never be able to identify anything as intangible or profound as human talent. An expert system could assemble data for a business plan, maybe even verify the data in the business plan, but it could not even pretend to contribute to strategy. Moreover, no responsible organization would ever cede so much control to the mysteries of machinery. No one would — or should — give up that much control.

Finally, opponents of expert systems will cap these arguments with two powerful observations. First, they will note that computer systems in general are notoriously unreliable. They crash for no known reason and resume also for no known reason. And that is quite apart from their vulnerability to sabotage, intrusion, and virus infection. The extensive use of expert systems would leave an organization wholly hostage to its computers, utterly fragile in the face of any systematic computer failure or malicious attack. For these reasons, the widespread use of expert systems is alleged to be an unrealistic fantasy.

However, if we look carefully at the facts of each of these arguments, an entirely different picture emerges. The starting point of the argument is quite correct, but the conclusions are faulty. Let us begin by looking more closely at the existing applications in industrial process control.

WHEN THE GENIE ESCAPES THE BOTTLE

Simply put, expert programs have two primary uses: they serve in those situations where human decision making is too slow to be practical, and they improve the quality of the human decision. The first applications traditionally involve manufacturing process and control, and many of these operations have fully integrated computer control systems. The program decides whether a valve opens or not, for example, and when the conveyer belt rolls. In many of these situations, the problems the expert rules are there to address are very straightforward and need only routine evaluation; the technical challenge is, for the most part, no more than the careful development of the interface and monitor controls. This trend to computer-assisted manufacturing (CAM) can be expected to grow. Of course, humans are being replaced not only because they're too slow, but also because they are too expensive.

Competition's need for rapid response is also pushing the use of expert systems out of the factory and into the distribution chain. Expert programs now order, schedule, and record the flow of inputs, even as they take orders, schedule, and ship end products. These demand/ supply-chain management programs are stitching together a seamless process, like taking a lump of iron and pacing it through multiple functions until it leaves the dealer's lot as part of a new car. The result is to bleed inventory out of the production process from almost all of its stages. Indeed, we are entering a phase where production does not begin until the customer has ordered (common already with personal computers and an approaching reality with cars). As a result, there is a large and continuing efficiency gain as the dead-weight cost of inventory is removed from society. In addition, the fulfilment of customer requirements is enhanced.

And while the drumbeat of competition has made a parts clerk too slow to satisfy the customer's request, another incidental benefit has resulted. Since inventory is too expensive to maintain, there are no longer buffer stocks available to absorb errors. As a result, shipments cannot be allowed to go astray and transport companies are forced to improve the quality of their services. This has an effect on all aspects of production, but none is more important than the effect on the quality of manufactured products. Each component has to be made right the first time, with a minimal defect rate. And at every step in the process or assembly, the same requirement applies: do it right or production slows to a halt. Or the customer's delivery date is missed, a deadly consequence in a highly competitive marketplace. The result for the customer is a better-quality product made with less cost.

It is difficult to overstate the economic effects produced by expert systems in process and distribution-control. The benefits are so great that it is nearly impossible to be a major manufacturer or distributor unless an expert system is being used. To fail to use these systems is to render the company utterly uncompetitive, and these tools have entered the marketplace with relative speed. It is particularly interesting to observe that while expert systems for manufacturing took a reasonable length of time to enter the marketplace, expert systems for distribution have been placed into widespread use much more quickly. This is, of course, not surprising, since the distribution programs are being implemented during a period when the competitive pressures are higher. Manufacturing introduced these systems somewhat more slowly a few years ago, when competitive pressures were less acute. This suggests that every new wave of innovation in expert systems will be forced into the marketplace at a faster pace than the previous waves.

We should also not underestimate the effect of precedent. Once any category of human decision making is systematically replaced, the next level of decisions are in the firing line. Once the factory manager's function has been subsumed, it becomes easier to turn to the next level of managerial decision making. One could argue that narrower problems are more easily addressed by expert systems (which is, of course, true), but that narrowness is itself a wholly arbitrary distinction. What is a broad task one day can look quite narrow the next day. The genie is truly out of the bottle, and nothing is going to put it back in.

THE STEEL-COLLAR WORKER

In effect, expert systems are infiltrating the economy in forms that are not always fully recognized. A particularly important example involves robotic applications. The robot's full programmability provides its defining characteristic: flexibility. By contrast, automated machines, which may or may not use computers or microprocessors, are marked by their inflexibility. Automated machinery, which dates back to the advent of the assembly line, has served society well by producing uniform goods at low cost. These machines gave to the mass market products that had once been available only to the elite in the form of customized hand-crafted goods. But automated machines (that is, automatic machines that run with minimal human supervision) come with one great disadvantage: they were designed to do just one thing very well. Whether the controlling feature was a "counting" cog or a microprocessor, there was no getting away from this basic inflexibility.

The robot is, even in its initial stage, far different (it should be noted that the industry's use of terms is inconsistent; some automated machines are called robotic when they are not). The robot is best described as the adaptable machine, because, with its computer brain, any new program provides a new set of functions. When there is a change in the environment, the robot adapts. And since humans also adapt, some robotic behaviour will mimic that of humans. The science-fiction writers have it partly right, even though they routinely violate all the laws of economics.

The economic benefits of robots as adaptable machines are difficult to overstate. Adaptability is the characteristic most demanded by the marketplace. Deliver that function and the market cannot fail to reward you. The capital cost of the adaptable machine can be spread out over many years as it responds to a wide range of customer preferences. Factories will no longer need downtime to retool (in other words, to rebuild their assembly lines and any automated machinery). Moreover, as robots become fully integrated into the production process, they will prove capable of much more than a quick response if consumers suddenly want more trucks. Eventually, they will build your vehicle exactly as you want it, with 500 or 1,000 variations. Indeed, they will be able to create a vehicle that is unique in any practical sense. And the marketplace will have come full circle: those expensive customized products for the elite, which were followed by inexpensive uniform products for the mass market, will finally be replaced by inexpensive customized products for everyone. The robot is the guild master of the new millennium.

But if robots are guild masters, they are also experts by definition. So they are already experts in picking, packing, inspecting, and welding. There is no reason to expect them to be content with their present lot, however. The adaptability of the robots will also allow them to enter industries from which they are presently absent. The service industries in general and household maintenance in particular are logical candidates as robots move off the shop floor and the loading dock, their natural first home. Health care, hospitality, insurance, recreation, and banking are all ripe for application. Quite correctly, banks speak of automated banking machines (ABMs), not robotic banking machines (RBMs). But the RBMs are coming. With their greater flexibility, they will be able to create and dispense any kind of banking document, from a loan agreement to a letter of credit, and also accept documentation of all kinds (to settle a disputed payment, for example). They will accept a million pennies, disgorge premium gifts, and hand out rewards. In the hospital, they will mix and dispense drugs, prepare food, and scrub floors. The hospitality robot will arrive with refreshments, ice, buttons, or toothbrushes. It will shine shoes and press pants. Insurance robots will file, sort, and move paper. The "rec" robot will help you improve your tennis game with unfailing patience. And the household-maintenance market is crying out for robotic helpers as millions of working couples struggle to keep a clean and organized home. Where there is repetition, there is the computer and its handmaiden, the robot.

Part of the reason that robots have not advanced even faster is that all too often they are being designed (or fitted) for human work. Often this process asks more flexibility than the technology currently allows. The more effective approach would design the work for the robot. Within the broader service economy, there are ample opportunities to redesign work for robotic capability. In many cases, this will involve a major overhaul of an organization's workflow and a basic reconsideration of what needs to be done. Unfortunately, many larger organizations find this type of restructuring very difficult, and for that reason, the first-generation robots for the service industries are often relegated to the mailroom or the print shop.

Companies that have expanded their robotic production have not always been satisfied with the results, and some have scaled back their efforts. For example, a few auto plants introduced robotic production, only to realize few apparent cost savings. While these seeming failures slow robotic development, they are an insufficient reason to reconsider the inherent benefits of robots. Moreover, they can be traced to clear causes. There is often a lack of appreciation for what the human worker does, and as a result, the robot falls short in some critical area. If a company wants to replace a human with a machine, it had better understand the human first. Also, robots have not always been integrated into the overall workflow carefully, and their present capabilities may have been oversold. These highly flexible machines need to be put to work in the arena for which they are *presently* best suited, especially as they are constrained by their own physical limitations.

The economic logic of the robot is too strong to deny, and thus we can confidently expect it to gain in acceptance. And while robots may be misused in some applications, the trend towards wide adoption will be spurred by a growing shortage of skilled labour of all kinds. Robots will replace people because, in many situations, people are more expensive. But there's an even stronger need for robots to replace humans who are not available. To a progressively greater degree, the robot will substitute for unavailable labour. For example, a shortage of highly experienced tool and die makers has necessitated the use of computer-controlled machinery that "knows" part of the job. Virtually any technical trade is open to this possibility. And if there is no one to service the machine, it either services itself or calls out to another machine. Thus the supply of skilled labour can be increased by the simple replication of a piece of software and the manufacture of a machine. The other option is to reproduce and educate a human being, a much longer and more uncertain process.

Robots, like all expert systems, can excel in areas where humans fall short. For example, with human employees, pride in work is often in relatively short supply. They, for example, seldom take pride in maintaining the hygiene of the workplace (that is, cleaning toilets). Robots have no such problem: their commitment is programmable. While there are men and women of quality who bring their own high standards to any task they perform, including workplace maintenance, these people are rare enough that we need the robot backstop.

Indeed, expert systems do more than just provide expertise — they also contribute steadfastness of purpose. They get neither distracted nor lazy, discouraged nor annoyed. Since clear-minded focus is such an important advantage for our robot welder, it is difficult to see that it would be of less importance to the manager or to any knowledge worker. In an expert system, motivation is captured in a few lines of code. There is no reason to believe that such a golden elixir will stay restricted to the assembly line for very long.

INTO THE EXECUTIVE SUITE

Expert systems have already left the shop floor and are steadily and stealthily advancing into high-level decision making. Those who object to expert systems are preparing to repulse a full frontal attack by these relentless rule-makers; it will be a conflict of a thousand decentralized skirmishes. Expert systems will eat their way into an organization, and across and up its decision-making ladder. There will be no quantum leaps, however; rather, the programs will learn their way up the decision tree to ever higher levels. The outcome is inevitable, with the expert systems building up a critical mass until they are finally too established to be resisted. They will have become a business norm step by irrevocable step, sometimes without anyone noticing.

In fact, the expert system is already firmly established in one of the marketplace's most critical and high-profile industries: finance. If the robot welder is the base of the economic value chain, the capital allocator is the top. And every business function in between is under siege. Middle managers are the meat of the sandwich in more ways than one.

There are a wide variety of computer programs that advisers at major financial institutions already use to choose their investments (these programs go well beyond the mechanical task of executing a trade). But because these "computer trading" programs are not referred to as the expert systems they are, many businesspeople fail to see them as such. Most of these trading systems use elaborate rules to guide them while they troll the world's financial marketplaces, identifying openings for arbitrage or hedging. They are, of course, essential to the execution of complex specialized securities, including the important category of derivatives. These trading programs are now so commonplace that they have set a precedent for the financial industry and elsewhere.

The expert trading systems were relatively easy to introduce, since many of the functions they execute cannot be performed by humans. Too often, the human trader is too slow to notice the opportunity, too slow to calculate the response, or too confused to see the opportunity in the blizzard of data. And since these programs work and make money, their adoption is assured. It is sure to happen quickly as well, since as soon as a competitor uses it, no other company can delay (or it will be on the losing end of every trade it makes).

Expert systems now also advise financial institutions on the credit-worthiness of customers and securities, using elaborate sets of rules to assess risk. The major credit card companies have, of course, long used these kinds of computerized rules to manage their vast client bases. It would have been impossibly expensive to manage so many accounts without them. The card companies also work feverishly to mine their databases for even better rules about which customers to solicit and which to ignore, who gets the higher credit limit and who does not. The rules affect everything from advertising to responses to telephone inquiries.

Capital One, for example, has become a powerful new presence in the credit card market, and it argues that its success came because it researched its market space more carefully than its competitors. This knowledge is embedded in Capital One's expert systems. Other companies have had to respond to this pressure, and as a result, the credit card market has become steadily more competitive. It is the forum of the battling software. And the competition produces, as we would easily anticipate, more pressure to implement improved and extended expert systems. What is happening in this marketplace will in due course happen everywhere.

The competitive situation is similar for those companies that use customer relationship management (CRM) and distribution-chain expert systems. In effect, a company's CRM software battles that of other companies, as does the distribution software. (If competing companies happen to be using the same uncustomized expert software from a third party, a more effective approach will soon occur to one of them, an approach that will only strengthen the role of the expert system.) It would be the height of naïveté to suggest that once expert systems have entered managerial decision making (as they already have), they will magically stop just one millimetre short of the executive suite. That, of course, assumes we suffer no disastrous computer crash.

MELTDOWN

The expert trading systems offer a clear example, it is argued, of the danger inherent in trusting too much work to the computer. There is a concern that as they gain more capability, these trading systems will have the potential to disrupt the capital markets severely. Some business-people worry about the effect on the marketplace of these programs working in combination. Perhaps, it is suggested, there are rare combinations of economic and market conditions that, together with the programs, would result in the failure to clear transactions. The programs might all try to sell or buy simultaneously, which could set off a cascade of consequences around the world that would cause confidence in the financial system to be greatly impaired. This is especially troubling for those who understand that without confidence, all the numbers in the financial system are rendered meaningless. Of course, if there is any serious market disruption, the financial industry and its developers will face the threat of governmental regulation to restrict the use of the systems.

The danger of such disruptions arises for several reasons. While the programs acting in concert could produce a market failure, there is no incentive for any financial company acting alone to address the difficulty. Any one company that found and fixed the danger would be making a gift to the entire industry. And the software companies aren't going to do it either; they are focused on satisfying their individual customers and their individual interests. Public agencies do monitor the markets, but they are unlikely to have the resources necessary to understand a complex set of mathematical relationships expressed in a computing program. In this situation, with a possible danger attracting insufficient attention, the likelihood grows of the danger actually occurring. And if the danger is centred on a procedure that very few in any given organization understand exactly, it is further magnified.

But that is only part of the problem. Beside systematic failure, there is an equal danger of intrusion. Crime can dependably be counted upon. White-collar thieving is rising, even as youth crime fades. There have never been more white-collar workers, with more access and more wealth to tempt. And thus never was there more value at greater risk. And tomorrow, each of these determinants of theft will mount yet again. Losses are already high (so high that they are often disguised), and there is no doubt they will get higher.

There is another threat that can be expected to grow. Rapid technological and economic change is convincing some people that society is actually regressing. Some of those who have decided that we are headed for apocalypse are so sure of their conviction that they view industrial sabotage as a valid, even responsible, tool for social action. And if sabotage in the twenty-first century means anything, it means attacking the establishment through its vital communication and computing networks. This is the ultimate threat, one rarely stated because it is so cataclysmic. All we need is a terrorist group whose members are smart enough to understand that instead of blowing up people or buildings, there is something else they can do.

Security is a problem that will never be solved. In fact, it is unrealistic, no matter how compelling the mathematics, to believe that data security can be addressed once and for all. After all, it is a multi-faceted (that is, multidisciplinary) issue. Even if the mathematics of the coding was flawless, the security process is vulnerable to the rogue insider, the careless user, weak documentation, and botched implementation. Security is the most subtle of games, part intellectual, part blocking mechanisms.

GUARDIAN LOCKSMITH

In spite of all those security concerns, however, the expert systems of the financial industry remain in place. Even though computers can fail, and even though failure within the financial system could have the most severe consequences, expert systems remain firmly entrenched. Indeed, the financial system itself is now no more than one elaborate and interconnected set of computers talking to each other about numbers. It is far too late to go back to paper. And ironically enough, this is a spur to the further development of the expert system; improved systems must be deployed to guard the computer establishment that is already in place.

For example, the trading programs invite the creation of disaster-prevention software that would take them off-line at the first discernible sign of systemic market failure. Once such a fail-safe program was operational, it would quickly find its way around the world, forging a guaranteed market with the probability of strong IP protection. Of course, such a program could not be developed without extensive R&D involving sophisticated mathematical analysis, dedicated and specialized search procedures, and conceptually keen insight. There would also be no guarantee of success, and extensive experimentation would be required, since there's no margin for error.

But once perfected, an expert system that made trading fail-safe would uncover other applications. The main strategies of this software could likely be translated into other disaster-control situations. As computer systems penetrate into more areas of the economy, the danger of systemic failure rises. While a sudden collapse of a program for supply-chain management is not likely to give rise to financial panic, it would cause (and has already caused) heavy financial losses. Hershey had just such an unfortunate incident when its new inventory software created so many disruptions that the company was unable to fill its Christmas orders. And because programs of different organizations are sometimes exchanging information, a collapse could have the same cascading effect as that of the financial programs. There are, of course, a wide range of critical computer functions that need expert fail-safe controls. So huge and profitable a market cannot be ignored.

Computer security is another lucrative market opportunity for expert software. The security system will create a tightly woven blanket of protection that will range from the lowly security guard (who had better not be lowly) to the senior executives (and their lovers). Security is, of course, essentially a human problem. Machines have never been known to sneak into a private place, steal, lie, and cheat; humans have.

So what is the response of the computer "security expert" (who is actually an encryption specialist) who is asked how the "system" will stop the vice-president of finance from taking the computers off-line for "emergency maintenance" the day before he flees to a jurisdiction with no extradition treaty? All too often this computer specialist shrugs and says that this possibility cannot be prevented, and that it is not the software's fault. But such a response is a misunderstanding of what the marketplace wants. The market wants protection from intrusion and theft. And if computer "experts" think that software cannot guard against the "human" problem, then they do not understand the true capability of the technology that they so like to celebrate. An expert security system will incorporate both the most advanced mathematical keys and the most recent and proprietary "security" calibrations. It will, yet again, take extensive and expensive research to develop and much time to construct. But the payoff justifies the effort.

The characteristics of such a system can be broadly sketched. The expert system would orchestrate and manage a full array of security tools, both electronic and non-electronic. There would be multiple, interrelated levels of security, including time lags and false keys, true locks and false locks, real doors and false doors. The system would continuously monitor the communication flow, both external and internal, looking for the characteristic patterns of general criminal behaviour and electronic crime. It would strip security-breaking decision making out of the organization chart, having identified the critical nodes, and it would actively maintain a chain of responsibility that leads directly to the CEO and the board of directors. There would be a fortified audit trail for all information that moves in and out of the organization. A hidden back channel would give senior management a continuing security overview. And some of the most critical functions will still be performed on computers that operate behind locked doors and are in no physical way connected to the world. In other words, the data will be moved by someone who uses a real key to open a real door.

But the critical point is that none of these security layers should be added merely because they seem logical. They must be designed specifically to address what actually happens during attempted intrusions. For example, a certain series of inquiries from one department might signal a potential intrusion; from another department, however, these inquiries might be perfectly benign. The volume of traffic in a particular channel or through a particular port might be another "mark" of criminal intent. And the system would be able to "remember" every recorded instance of a lapse in security; this memory would be triggered every time there was a computer or communication system upgrade. And of course, the security system would continually add new protection features. Special care will have to be taken to integrate the security system with the rest of the organization's information technologies, also on a continuing basis. Of course, none of this is a guarantee against theft or intrusion; measures like those described above can only reduce its likelihood. But that is why such expert systems will remain so important a commercial opportunity. And why they will serve as a clear inspiration to expert developers of other applications.

MARIONETTE OR NOT?

Expert systems are indispensable to modern management precisely because executives and managers need to be able to sift through and evaluate a mass of continually changing data and accommodate qualitative or intangible considerations. As we have observed, information is out of control, its weight a burden on us all. And yet, most businesses do not have an adequate information or knowledge strategy. They do not understand the hierarchy of data, which starts with information and progresses through knowledge to wisdom. They do not know what information is incorrect, who has the information, who should have the information, or how to find or create the information that provides competitive advantage. Fortunately, these are all problems for which expert systems are precisely designed and particularly well suited.

While larger organizations often have something called a knowledge strategy, or even a knowledge manager, this is usually a preliminary, limited, or rhetorical approach. And millions of smaller businesses — the majority of companies — do not even pretend to have such strategies. The norm is crisis management, which is hardly surprising when the culture of business still extols action over research or learning. But as expert systems — the ultimate knowledge tool — force themselves on business, the bias towards mindless action will be set aside. Competition demands that the right information be used by the right person at the right time and place. And the expert system delivers exactly that.

The fact that some information is hard to quantify does not minimize the role of the expert systems. First, the expert system will insist that intangibles are accepted only after there has been an exhaustive search for quantitative data or appropriate proxies. All too often, a qualitative observation is an excuse for a lack of analytic rigour. Or it is intended merely as a ruse to promote one opinion over another.

Where there are qualitative variables that are genuine, as there are, the expert system will insist that they be heeded. Even though the value of a company's reputation for integrity (or the pure elegance of a design, or the safety of a child) is not subject to precise measurement, it is the role of the expert system to guarantee that intangible does not become synonymous with unimportant. The expert system will insist that any special characteristics be taken into account during the decision-making process.

The critic will finally insist that the fundamental objection to the expert system is its rule base. Since the expert system is nothing but a set of rules, this observation strikes to the heart of the technology. Indeed, the critic argues that there is a logical point beyond which the expert system should not advance, even if it is not now precisely clear where that line is. This line of reasoning is based on the fact that society and its marketplaces are, in the final analysis, an expression of the human experience. It is an experience both fluid and flexible, pulsating with energy and idiosyncratic nuance. It flows into unexpected pathways, encountering the genius of inspiration and the synergy of luck. While rules can apply here to some degree, it's true that they are utterly hostile to the fundamental nature of human society — to its creative spark, its restlessness, its stranger moods and interesting backwaters. To impose an elaborate rule set, the argument goes, is to put us all in a smothering straitjacket. Such a tyranny of expert rules would either be swept aside in something approaching rebellion or gut individual initiative and possibly the very spirit of human life.

This argument deserves to be taken seriously. Part of it is the age-old argument that it is better to dance naked in the firelight to appease the storm gods than it is to learn to build a shelter. Resistance to the learned response is quite often an excuse to avoid the painful exercise of learning. It is, of course, true that the learned response is often wrong. But this observation can justify only a new search for the truth, not the celebration of the random impulse.

Yet even so, humanity is not a rule machine. Indeed, it is for this reason that humans do not follow rules especially well. Therefore, without a doubt, there are arenas into which expert systems should not go (even though some of them will, with predictably horrendous results). The point of the expert system is to apply rules in situations where the rules are known, to apply them to problems with established and proven answers. But rules should never be applied to the unusual circumstance. If a powerful new competitor or an alternative technology suddenly appears in the marketplace, the human manager must take the lead. The same should happen if sales inexplicably plummet or financial performance takes a nose-dive. If anything is going significantly wrong, the expert system is obviously out of its depth. The expert system should never assume the manager's responsibility to deal with exceptional situations. That is exactly — and *only* — what managers should exist to do.

The expert system performs routine functions well, and management involves a large measure of routine, repetitious work that is just waiting to be performed by machine — hire employees, fire employees, take orders, fill orders, balance the books, issue cheques, and so on. Even allowing for varied circumstances, many of these activities have a common repetitive core.

With expert systems, managers will be freed to do only the interesting work: addressing exceptions, revisiting and revising company strategy, uncovering opportunities and identifying threats. We'd like to believe that everyone would prefer this kind of work, instead of reading yet one more memo about travel expenses. Yet for the timid and the untrained, non-routine work will be intimidating.

The value of the expert system extends from several sources. It will not forget relevant factors, an all-too-common event in frantic and understaffed organizations (that is, most organizations). It will be able to implement a new procedure or advance in understanding speedily and effectively. As companies adapt with swiftness to changed conditions, they also force their competitors to respond. And thus the competitive pressure of the marketplace increases yet again. That forces more productivity and more prosperity, and spurs the development of new and better expert programs.

The most important benefit of the expert system is its ability to provide managers with that most valuable resource: time to think. The crisis-ridden atmosphere of most organizations is the enemy of coherent thought. Indeed, it is amazing that more organizations do not suffer failures and fiascos, given how little quality time is available to their managers at any level. While senior management tries to delegate the routine tasks to the level below, there are enough routine errors there to endlessly distract them. And on the few occasions that the senior managers try to map basic strategy, they are in the position, whether they recognize it or not, of needing the knowledge of their junior managers, who are so busy dealing with the routine crises that they are in no position to give it. If the CEO is a genius, everything is fine until that person retires. But if the CEO is only a normally competent person, the organization is doomed to stumble forward, sometimes into opportunity and sometimes into disaster. The expert systems allow all of the management staff to focus on thinking and planning for the future. Of course, this ultimately means many fewer managers, or so it is argued. But can there ever be enough people trying to peer into the future, trying to see what is not there but could be? Can we ever have too many people trying to create new solutions in this dark and primitive world?

Expert systems are certainly about control. And there is little doubt that these systems can be used to malevolent ends. But there is also little doubt that they can be used to unleash human talent to a degree beyond that of any other technology.

CHAPTER EIGHT

CONTROL AND MEMORY

DELEGATE INTO CHAOS

As soon as a business is of any significant size, the "boss" begins to lose control. This is so inevitable that it is turned into a virtue. Executives are told to delegate, to trust the capabilities of others in order to create a successfully growing enterprise. While that is good advice, it obscures the problems of control and accountability, both of which expert systems address.

As most organizations grow, their energies are dispersed: activities of questionable value proliferate, efforts are duplicated, private agendas and political chicanery mount, initiatives fly off in every direction. In the process, the company's focus is diffused and its principal competitive advantage can erode. And in spite of all the memos, manuals, organizational charts, and exhortations to the contrary, this tendency endures. By contrast, the expert system allows the CEO to invite initiative and effort where it is wanted, to prevent it from being used where it is not, and to insist that the effort be disciplined.

Expert systems deliver control over expertise, which is information in its most highly applicable form. While this is most often about control over the marketplace, it is no less about control over people. The issue of control is often overlooked, sometimes intentionally. In today's culture, control over the individual, especially control by the machinery of Big Brother, is suspect. But the expert system provides the means to control individual behaviour, whether that's politically correct or not. In this sense, an expert system is a powerfully seductive management tool.

From monarch to chief executive officer, the lust for control, more nakedly called power, remains strong. Thus it is not hard to imagine that the push to adopt expert systems will be driven in large measure by senior executives; middle managers will resent these systems, even as they impose them on those reporting to them. Or rather, this resentment will come when it is more widely recognized that organizational control is a clear consequence of expert systems. (Organizational control is a more gentle way of describing control over people.)

But it is easy to see how this capacity for control could produce catastrophic results in the hands of a power-hungry executive. Still, control is an entirely necessary function for any organization. The bigger the organization, the greater the need for control (this is, after all, what contributes to common purpose and the efficient use of resources). Without control, there is an inevitable tendency to chaos as any organization grows. Moreover, it must be emphasized that for a wide range of commercial activities, from automobile manufacturing to banking, large-scale production is necessary. Economies of scale do exist, and they directly contribute to society's standard of living. Therefore, control, to the extent that it helps large organizations capture these economies of scale, directly serves society.

Whether it's acknowledged or not, control remains a key concern of all organizations. The amount of resources devoted to ensuring control makes this clear. There are the reams of reports written, reviewed, and discussed; the budgets set, monitored, and modified; the meetings that go on towards an ever-receding horizon. While many meetings are genuine attempts to develop collaborative solutions, at least an equal number are merely about communicating a decision, discussing why the decision is not being executed, or arguing about why someone thinks it is being executed and someone else thinks it is not.

Communication, that function that uses up so much scarce time, is as much about asking someone what we should do as it is about telling them what they should do. Or stated more precisely, it is both these things in a blend that is often misunderstood (was that a command, a question, or a suggestion?).

Most organizations merely reflect the reality of the society of which they are a part. Decisions themselves are often flawed, and there is no reason to think that the process of executing flawed decisions is any more effective than the process that produced the decision itself. Decisions are not communicated dependably (no one told me) or to the appropriate person (that is not my job), and of course, information gets lost as it moves up and down the organizational ladder. The number of chief executives who issue memos that never seem to deliver results is beyond counting. Think not? How many CEOs "demand" that their companies lower costs or increase profits and receive no response? The failure is, of course, easily dismissed as a result of the inevitable uncertainties of the marketplace or the inadequacy of the workers. But there is often another explanation: the specific instructions never arrived. Or they arrived, but there was no way to enforce them (or notice that they were not being enforced).

Large organizations, like armies, need to have orders clearly issued and reliably followed. In a fluid situation where this may or may not be occurring, there can be little accountability. The battle was lost, but who is to blame? Where there is no accountability, the power of management is severely impaired. In many of today's organizations, it is difficult to bestow blame or give credit *accurately*. (The blame and the credit are assigned, nevertheless, because they must be.) In all too many cases, there is not even a record of who tried to make or evade the decision.

The Dilbert cartoon is popular because it is an exaggeration of reality, not a distortion of it.

NOTHING LOST

The above observations are no more than a reiteration of the inherent difficulties of management. People are hard to control — that is, manage — and business schools exist to suggest ways to improve management techniques. Expert systems are, in effect, no more than an advanced and more powerful management tool. They provide their control across many levels. First, expert systems manage the flow of information within an organization. Instead of lazily replicating the typical corporate e-mail distribution system (where everyone gets practically everything), the expert system analyzes information flow and recommends an improved process. It is then an easy step to have this process automatically adjust itself. Let's say, for example, that a company launches a new expanded marketing initiative. With an expert system, information flow will be altered to accommodate this changed set of circumstances. Now extra information will flow from marketing to manufacturing and inventory control.

On the other hand, if the company was trying to accelerate an R&D project, the information flow would be different. Perhaps information should flow not to marketing but to human resources to trigger more recruitment. Or maybe more information should go to corporate strategic planning and less to financial controls. In other words, there are changes not only in content, but also in volume and distribution points. Moreover, such a system could easily alert management to any significant change in the composition of the information flow. Within a global financial institution, for example, a sudden surge in the information traffic to Japan might signal either opportunity or danger. It is far from convincing when a corporation extols "the strategic importance of information" without even knowing who knows what in real time and making no effort to analyze knowledge flow over time. It is not redundant to note that anything is doomed to be lost when nobody knows where anything is.

Expert systems will track the flow of information and document the repositories of data. Moreover, the systems will *require* the archiving of information, for without archives it is impossible to reconstruct any event. What is not recorded cannot be a lesson learned (and that means retained for more than a quarterly report). But the properly designed expert system will make it practical to learn and to *insist* that this occur.

NOWHERE TO HIDE

In effect, an expert system of any kind can be used to ensure compliance. Without such systems, rule enforcement is entirely sporadic. This is hardly surprising, given that such enforcement is time-consuming (and rarely anyone's sole responsibility) and naturally resented by many employees. The computer, by contrast, has the time and capacity, and it is immune to boredom and resentment. Thus the second function of the expert system is to act as a tool for compliance that can be used with various degrees of stringency. The expert program will know whether file A was sent by the head of marketing to the head of R&D, as well as whether the file was opened by the recipient. It will know that the subject of the file was mandated. And it will archive the file so that its contents can be consulted or reviewed at any time in the future. The system, using its own rules to decide which records will be kept and which will not, addresses the great cliché that victory has a thousand fathers and defeat is an orphan. In other words, it will not let either the victors or the vanquished write their own history. Nothing about such a system is in any way technically impossible.

The compliance capability of the expert system can be applied to any kind of corporate function. Already a variety of organizations use the computer to enforce specific requirements by programming it to stop a process unless a particular step has been completed. While the approach is not particularly elegant, it can be highly effective. For example, bank employees processing credit applications on-line will discover that they cannot proceed unless all the information fields have been filled. This is, of course, intended to prevent an application from going forward with incomplete information. This example would be even more impressive if some of the information fields were not irrelevant, and if the bank employee was not forced into typing gibberish into some of the fields to allow the on-line system to continue to function. Of course, a correctly designed expert system would have the flexibility to accommodate different requirements depending on what was or was not relevant to a particular client file. Moreover, a true expert system would actually detect the gibberish being entered into the field. A compliance tool for credit management is not particularly effective when there is no quality control on the information being entered. Similar examples exist in a variety of other business applications. It is clear how far we yet have to go before information is treated as the precious commodity it truly is.

Such systems of compliance can certainly be seen to be "intrusive," however. The employee who wants autonomy and responsibility will object to this level of monitoring. But the dilemma is quite clear: if information is power (and it is), then a corporation actually has a fiduciary responsibility to control that information, exactly as it does its finances. The corporation has an obligation to know what has or has not happened and to maintain a record of each and every real transaction, just as it should do for its financial transactions. While there certainly are employees who will find it annoying or insulting to have to defer to information controls as they defer to budgets and other financial controls, a responsible corporation has little choice but to require that this be done. After all, the financial numbers are a mere subset of information in its totality. And as this becomes widely recognized, the age of information will take on at least some meaning. It is a rare employee who does not understand the need for financial controls, but most employees will have to be taught that in the evolving life of the corporation, information will now take on equal value.

This means information about everything. All workers at all levels must accept that they will always have a computerized expert system standing at their shoulder (or looking over their shoulder). These systems will appear as both ally and taskmaster. There is no doubt whatsoever that this will produce a more challenging workplace for everyone from the clerk to the senior executive. The worker at all levels is being asked more and more often to defer to the machine. This will be stressful, and the workers will not always be clear about what residual tasks have been left to them. But this is exactly the effect that mounting competition produces: work becomes harder. And if workers find it stressful when the expert system demands that a piece of information be considered or saved, they will find it even worse when the expert system is asking for results.

Part of the stress on the worker can be addressed by that simple and crude admonition to "get over it." But in some ways, it's much more complicated than that, especially since it's often a question of attitude. There are among us workers who prefer the shadows, who like to work in the background without the pressure of constant supervision. They try to justify their lack of self-confidence, experience, commitment, or pride in work as a desire to be free. But it's an argument they often do not believe themselves. There are also more assertive workers, those who do not shrink from the limelight. They have the confidence to be tested every day, to believe that if a mistake comes to light, they will just fix it fast. They will tend to see the expert system as a tool for even greater accomplishment. Of course, the latter group of workers will find that they have to live up to their brave words, while those workers who are less comfortable to begin with will surely struggle to adjust. Any corporation that understands that it needs human workers (some will start doubting that as the expert systems advance) will also recognize that the timid worker can learn both skill and confidence, can grow into someone capable of wielding expert systems in the pursuit of profitable accomplishment. Unfortunately, that is not always the corporate response. All too often, firms will simply try to find or steal more information warriors, those men and women who see information as a competitive weapon and can wield it with passion. They will often look in vain.

MEMORY THAT NEVER SLEEPS

As the marketplace becomes more dynamic, corporate memory must be enhanced. Today the histories of the planet's major business organizations and their creation of technology are almost unknown and will remain so. Most of the records are gone; most of the players are dead. The histories that do exist represent a mere fraction of the world's political histories, even of those societies that are much smaller and less influential than the world's leading corporations. There are presidential libraries in the United States but not corporate ones, an anomaly that belies our claim to be a literate society.

Without memory, there can be no control of either the corporation or its destiny. Without an organized way to remember, a company cannot make informed choices about any market situation. It does not know, in any complete or formal sense, what it did that worked or did not work in the past. The same mistake is repeated again and again, while the successes of the past are ignored. This is hardly surprising when retirees are given a gold watch instead of a debriefing, when new employees read brochures instead of company histories, and when legal reporting requirements or storage costs, instead of the needs of the marketplace, are the deciding factor in whether or not to retain documents. With expert systems, by contrast, the past successes of the company are built into its very fabric. What worked in the past can be neither forgotten nor ignored, and each success is added to this digital fund of knowledge, a fund that is without limit and beyond fatigue.

THE EMBODIED CORPORATION

Expert systems marshal information, capture corporate memory, and facilitate compliance — which are, of course, all interconnected activities. Each supports the other, and together they give expert systems yet another dimension. An array of expert programs, carefully deployed, defines the company's structure, logic, procedures, and fundamental market orientations, and does so with a precision that no other technique can match.

The importance of this function cannot be underestimated. Expert systems create structure first by pacing a worker through almost any task. This responsibility goes well beyond their ability to induce compliance for specific, discrete tasks. That function can easily be expanded to include shepherding a worker through a complex series of interrelated steps, to produce a result that itself is connected to another stream of activity. At a conceptual level, this is no different from factory workers who are paced by an assembly line that drags work into their view; it is no different from the call-centre representative who reads off a script. It is essentially the act of giving structure to a piece of work — so it gets accomplished in a certain way to a certain effect. The only difference is that the expert system paces the worker through a much more elaborate chain of activity.

Consider the challenge of integrating two companies when one is acquired by or merged with the other. This is a common problem, and experience makes clear that the results range from excellent to disastrous. The stress at DaimlerChrysler, for example, is painful to watch. And since some companies, especially in the information industry, base their growth strategy on the aggressive acquisition of others, the failure of the integration process can call the entire logic of the enterprise into question.

This situation is ideal for the expert system. Integration is a complex, multi-faceted process, and one small mistake can be fatal (say, the acquired company's R&D talent leaves en masse). Different kinds of companies can be integrated in different ways, but many companies lack executives with experience in large-scale integration. Even companies with experienced teams of integration specialists are hostage to the sudden departure of several key members.

With an expert system, the company can specify *exactly* what kind of integration approach it wants. It can make sure no step is omitted (for example, by keeping vitally important employees happy during the transition), and it can set priorities. By pacing the tasks in sequence, the expert system can decide that retaining the acquired company's customers is a more important priority than integrating the IT systems or the financial controls (if it actually is). In fully developed expert systems, the pacing is not simply a matter of specifying that task A comes before task B. Rather, it's about identifying question A, the answer to which determines what the next action should be. Taken together, these questions and answers determine the company's integration policy. Again, there is no reason to see this as an impossible task.

In effect, the expert system is simply going through a very elaborate checklist, a sophisticated root-and-branch decision tree. It is not clear that it would be too complicated to overwhelm the calculating capacity of a large mainframe. And it cannot possibly be true that management could not actually specify all the steps in the process. (One would not like to believe that corporations are engaged in complex activity that they cannot even describe in a rigorous fashion.)

The International Standards Organization (ISO) quality-certification process is built exactly on the assumption that if you are doing something effectively, you will certainly have a record of how you do it and what benchmarks you use to determine that you have done it. Thus the ISO's certification procedure does not accept that a company can deliver quality if it cannot explain in precise detail how it goes about the process. Indeed, the ISO asks for a procedural manual and an audit protocol (which is, of course, an expert system in its bare bones). In the process of developing the ISO documentation, the company may very well discover that some things are left undone because there is no procedure in place to define them. In addition, this exercise often reveals activities that are simply falling through the cracks. Thus, of course, the intellectual exercise of creating the expert system is also likely to redefine the work itself, rather than merely describing what is happening (since what is happening is too experiential and improvised).

But we will also hear that even though pacing workers is a well-established practice in manufacturing, it will not work for every worker, especially knowledge or managerial workers. They will, it is claimed, not like such pacing. Of course, it is true that pacing has been applied most relentlessly to the repetitive tasks of shop-floor workers and some service workers, and less so to more "professional" work. Certainly the use of expert systems to pace professional work would require the workers to work differently, and to learn new responses in this changed situation. We will not be surprised to note that many workers find the change threatening, and thus they undertake it with considerable reluctance.

But one would hardly suggest that management resist change because workers do not like it. Or is the argument really to resist it because it is the *managerial* workers who are objecting? One would have thought that it was management's role to explain and implement change, to insist on its necessity. The logic driving expert systems is the same as that behind any advancing technology. And as in other cases, the technology may be slowed, but it will not ultimately be deflected, no matter how many people feel overwhelmed.

WRITE (CODE) IT DOWN

The importance of giving exact form to the basic strategic directions of an organization can hardly be underestimated. For example, many companies extol the virtues of human talent and claim this gives them their competitive advantage. They say that they prize and nurture this or that talent, that they welcome initiative and believe in employment equity. In most cases, this will be an honest statement of policy. But is this resulting in any different procedures than would have been the case without such a statement of policy? The answer from the CEO is yes, but it is usually difficult to determine in what way and to what degree. With the rigorous discipline of an expert system, however, a senior executive can ask a subordinate to explain how procedures have been modified or priorities redefined. Or the subordinate can be asked to explain how the specifics of the expert system, the procedural checklist, relate to the corporate intention. If people are a company's greatest asset, exactly what does this mean *operationally?*

Many companies claim they highly value employees with initiative. Yet they never seem to follow through on this claim, at least according to applicants to many of these companies. Clearly, the statement of belief has not been operationalized; in other words, it is not computable. But this does not mean that there is no expert system that can apply to or be created for this purpose. It should be noted that the expert system does not itself have to measure initiative, but it can insist that somebody else try to measure it in some way that creates an information track. This is no more than the engineer's argument that if you cannot specify it, you cannot make it. If it cannot be specified, it will not happen reliably.

From the loading dock to the boardroom, the documentation that would precede the creation of an expert system will find all manner of undone work, inconsistently done work, and unnecessary work. The discipline generated by this documentation alone is a powerful argument in favour of the implementation of expert systems. Upon examination, we will often find that there are no organized procedures for marketing to co-ordinate with engineering, for maintenance to co-ordinate with scheduling, for New York to co-ordinate with Toronto. We will discover there are no procedures in place to make sure that the latest market research is read, that an abnormality in the booking of sales is noticed. We will realize that there is no organized way to know that the number of complaints about a particular brand of tire has been expanding at an abnormal rate. Time and again, we will find that the procedures we assumed were in place are in fact absent. Other procedures that once were in place have atrophied, so they are no longer effective. And some of the procedures that are in place are no long relevant.

All this is in addition, of course, to the procedures that nobody is bothering to monitor. How many safety policies are being violated? one might naturally wonder. Too often we accept the argument that if we actually followed procedure, we could not get the work done. That, of course, is a justification for changing the procedure, not evidence that we should make up our minds chaotically. Only an inexperienced observer of the business community would doubt that these anomalies and difficulties exist, and that they are quite common. (Of course, we do not know how common because the massive documentation that would be necessary is absent; this is exactly the heart of the problem.)

ANOTHER APPROACH?

In spite of the prevalence of these difficulties, and in spite of the acknowledgement that it might be useful to discover where talk has not been translated into work, there can be a great reluctance to embrace expert systems. A variety of alternatives are suggested. Workers and managers could be educated or trained. Techniques to encourage initiative and job satisfaction could be implemented. Different forms of organization, often flatter and less hierarchical, are possible. While these might all be improvements, they do not deal with the central issues: flawed information, and bored and tired workers. And even though these suggestions have been often implemented in the past, they have not prevented a continuing series of corporate blunders and billions of dollars of lost investor value. The above alternatives have not prevented the dot-com fiasco or the wild thrashing about of the telecommunication companies and their equipment suppliers.

A somewhat more persuasive approach suggests that companies could be broken into relatively small, autonomous units; these units would then negotiate with each other, working out a variety of relationships. This presumes that something like a marketplace could be created within large companies to mitigate the need for control. The internal marketplace could control itself exactly as the overall external marketplace does. But while this avenue offers some intriguing possibilities, it is not applicable to every type of large-scale venture; it works best in a large organization that offers a wide range of products and services, like General Electric. Moreover, this approach does not address the fact that even the external marketplace fails because of flawed decision making and/or flawed execution. And even if control is not a problem, the need to improve decision making applies at all levels and to any size organization.

It is not unrealistic to suppose that the dot-com fiasco of the early days of this century could have been minimized by the more widespread use of expert systems. Indeed, the overreactions of investors and the consequent burst bubble were the result of flawed decision making, not some inevitable "psychological" excess. Imagine the effect of an expert system that reminded everyone — investors and management — of *everything* that has to be done to create a successful venture, and of *everything* that has to be done to evaluate an investment or a technology. Surely it is not implausible to suggest that you could slow people down by reminding them how many steps lie between small revenue and large revenue, and between revenue and profit. Of course, this would not have fully prevented the overreaction, but any degree of minimization could have saved a significant amount of resources.

Of course, greed causes people to ignore evidence. But the expert systems would make it difficult for them to do so. At the world's leading financial institutions, expert investment systems could be made mandatory, which would make them impossible to ignore, except at very great effort *and* as a matter of record. The memory of the expert system is itself a powerful spur to reasoned judgement. (Or should we suppose that the highly educated people in these institutions do not believe in the scientific method, in the validity of the very degrees they hold?)

FROZEN IN TIME, OR RULED BY A DESPOT?

A critic of expert systems might grant the above beneficial effects but still view them as not worth the long-run cost. There remains the fundamental objection that by codifying and mandating past practice, expert systems will trap us all in the past. Indeed, it is not difficult to see how this might take a society that is conservative and render it even less adaptable than it already is. Expert systems might further gut individual initiative, an attribute many believe is already in short supply. We should surely abstain from this technology, the argument goes, if it means making humans incapable of independent thought, helpless without a machine to tell them what to do or think next.

These dangers do assuredly exist. And while they can never be eliminated, they can at least be minimized. For instance, the creators of expert systems and their allied consultants can caution against undue rigidity and use training sessions to reinforce the point. But the better answer is to build limitations directly into the expert system. It is fundamental to the logic of the expert system that it must recognize when the situation it faces is exceptional and therefore outside its range of rules. At such a juncture, the system should demand human attention and disengage.

Unfortunately, management does sometimes attract people who are interested in neither the joy of accomplishment nor the challenge of battle; instead, these people are enamoured of the exercise of raw power. These petty tyrants will inevitably be attracted to expert systems, which they can use to impose fierce rigidity on their employees. They are likely to use expert systems to issue new orders for no better reason than to watch the troops "dance." Board members will have their work cut out for them in this situation, assuming they have a heart for it. Indeed, one of a board's first responsibilities will be to oversee the appropriate use of the expert system.

Expert systems, like all powerful technologies, are clearly open to abuse. While they can be used to create an inflexible structure, this response is self-defeating. Fortunately, in a tumultuous environment, a rigid structure is doomed to fail, although at great collateral cost. Put a company in a straitjacket and the next turning of the marketplace will leave it marooned.

FOCUSED INITIATIVE

But control does not necessarily imply rigidity; rather, control can be used to produce accomplishment. Intention is the key factor. Memory can be used to stop progress or to serve as a foundation for further advance. That is the responsibility of the decision-maker.

Expert systems can be used, if a company so chooses, to create an organization that *effectively* pursues its chosen goals. It does ask that all effort be applied to that purpose, that all information be saved and used. But interestingly enough, it also allows an organization to change quickly. By contrast, a large organization without expert systems changes slowly. With expert systems, a company can be "reprogrammed" much more quickly and effectively. Instead of meetings, conferences, new manuals, and endless memos, the organization now has its expert system directly tutoring the employee in a new set of responses. The army is now literally marching to the beat of a new drummer.

Of course, these new instructions are not always correct, and it is still possible for the reoriented company to make a major mistake. But that is then the fault of the senior managers, and they are held accountable; they have no one else to blame. That is real flexibility, with the decision-maker visible and thus responsible.

But there are dangers in having one person, or even a small group of people, deciding the fate of any major organization. This would be true even if the senior managers were well tutored by their own executive expert systems. With the structured framework of an expert system, however, it should be possible to require initiative *throughout* the organization, to build in discussion and debate, to mandate collaborative ideas. This is just another version of a checklist. What assumptions did you challenge today? What procedures should be approved? What is the company's newest danger? What new idea do you suggest? Where do *you* think the next opportunity will be found? These are difficult questions, and we shall see in the next chapter that there are expert systems to aid this process of innovation. But expert systems are quite capable of insisting on the function. Fortunately, by taking routine matters away from the managers, the expert system allows them time to use their initiative. When people don't have adequate time to think, it is futile to ask for independence of thought.

KNOW THYSELF

We must treat with respect the profound unease that many people will feel as expert systems bear down on them. They represent a radical change in the essential nature of work. Computing is finally going to have the transformational effect so long anticipated and so much misunderstood. Human society has not been turned upside down by spreadsheets, word processors, cheap communications tools, or computer games with cool graphics. And that's no surprise. Transformation is not likely to be caused by machines that are no more than appliances.

But computational power *can* have a revolutionary effect; it can change the very definition of who we are.

Expert systems will certainly redefine our work identity. But to many people, this is an intimately disturbing threat. With one technology, so much shifts — education, work, corporate governance, and investment opportunities. Before expert systems, aspiring professional workers had a clear pathway. All they needed was an education that would enable them to undertake a set of complex tasks. Over time, this set of tasks narrowed as the complexity rose. And even though that process could not go on indefinitely, it was a familiar and reassuring progression. But since expert systems address only complex problems, knowledge workers will find that they cannot use the mastery of complexity as their career advantage. Since workers must now deliver creative questions and innovative solutions, it is by no means certain that an education in complex tasks is particularly relevant.

Many people expect that the number of employees will fall as the computer eats into normal work. It has indeed been suggested that we are approaching the end of work, and this is why so many people fear what lies ahead. But this fear is understandable only in the context of our society's distorted view of work. As machines do more and more work, it is taken for granted that less work for humans remains. This idea is reinforced by the belief that humans do not have any inherent advantages over machines. (The apostles of high AI quite frequently hint at this idea, if they do not actually make the argument.) In addition, it is assumed that the amount of work on this planet is finite. This is an utterly implausible belief, given the want and distress that surrounds us every day.

The real problem is the unstated belief of many people that they are incapable of the creative response. If there is no need for them to do non-creative, repetitive work, they assume they will be unemployed. So, of course, by eliminating repetitive work, the expert systems are harbingers of declining employment opportunities. The lack of confidence most people have in their ability to engage in independent thought, to deal with situations they have not encountered before, is pervasive and disturbing. It is, therefore, utterly peculiar that expert systems are so often criticized for lessening the need for human initiative. It is almost as if we want to be independent, even though we do not have much confidence in our ability to act independently. Perhaps the knowledge that we could do something innovative substitutes for the actual need to do so. But it is strangely inconsistent to be told that expert systems will not work because of the need for human initiative. If human initiative is so critically important, then why do we fear the shortage of work? The answer is that in the old economy, we could avoid choosing whether to be innovative or imitative; this choice cannot be so easily avoided in the really new economy.

Given how unsure people are about what work they should and could actually do, it is completely understandable that they are uncertain. This uncertainty about innovative competence then crashes into the unblinking stare of the expert system's accountability function. By tracking who did what and what resulted, the expert system adds an entirely different type of stress to the mix. Of course, expert systems represent a challenge to everyone: they ask for a creative skill that seems difficult to deliver, and then they make it impossible to hide in the innards of the organization.

NO BREATHING SPACE

This transition to expert systems might still be tolerable if we could assume that it would proceed slowly. History teaches us that humans can adapt to radically new situations if they have sufficient time. But technology advances with impersonal force and accelerating speed. It is, therefore, unlikely that we will have the time we would like to get used to expert systems. Indeed, their rapid expansion is overdue, for all the reasons we have already discussed.

Unfortunately, this means that potential expert systems are building up, and when they finally move forward, they are likely to do so with startling speed. It will be like a log-jam breaking, exactly the experience society would like to avoid. The force that sets off this thunderous bumping and grinding will be the relentless pressure of competition.

And any economic slowdown will merely force companies into an even more frenzied struggle for profit. The stock markets have stopped funding non-performance, and companies must now use every means at their disposal to increase the rate of return. Competition will make it progressively harder for the stock markets to ignore limited financial performance.

THE LAMENT

It must be acknowledged that there are some workers who, because of circumstances or conditions over which they have no control, will not be able to make a successful transition to the new world of work. For example, the strength of economic advantage will push robotic development ahead rapidly. But as the robots advance into the workplace, they will inevitably replace many low-skilled, low-wage workers. In fact, the absolute number of low-skill workers is already falling in North America.

At today's pace of development, low-skilled, cheap labour anywhere on earth is in peril. It is not difficult to imagine that in several decades, no one will do unskilled work better or more cheaply than a robot. This is desirable, however, in the sense that we should not lament the decline of "dumb" work. But the disruption and deprivation that may result could be horrific. The future is a workplace where the only work available is that truly worthy of the human mind; unfortunately, many people will find themselves unable to rise to the challenge, in the industrial world and elsewhere. Even the rich industrial world, with its relatively few unskilled workers, will struggle to adjust; the poorer societies could be on the edge of disintegration.

In effect, we could end up hurting the most disadvantaged and vulnerable members of society. There is no easy way to avert this, but the worst thing we can do is fail to consider alternatives. Surely it is unacceptable merely to watch. Or perhaps we should say that we hope it will *become* unacceptable. Fortunately, the effectiveness of the expert systems is adding to our collective productive capacity — part of which could be directed towards helping those in distress . . . should we so choose.

THE IRONY

In spite of all these difficulties, expert systems will advance into the workplace; indeed, their progress is fundamentally irresistible. In what is not the least of the ironies of this situation, there is a strong subculture among developers that is aggressively libertarian. They decry every form of government intervention. They revel in their belief that the Internet's ability to move money anonymously will erode society's tax base. They advocate absolute free speech and tolerate no "censorship." They see the Internet as the foundation of a liberated community, a community free from interference by any governmental body. Yet computing, although it is indispensable to the Internet, is simultaneously creating an unambiguous instrument of organizational control. While these self-described rebels worship the Internet, the enemy advances on them from the rear. Whether they will make a sensible reply or merely command the tides to stop is open to debate.

CHAPTER NINE

IMPROVEMENT OR INNOVATION

TO GO WHERE NO ONE HAS GONE BEFORE

The full effect of expert systems on the business world can be seen only if we adopt the widest view of both computing and work. The principal effect of the computer on the nature of work is to eliminate the routine or repetitive procedure, whether physical or mental. Computer programs continue to advance through the hierarchy of work, gobbling up repetitive functions wherever they find them. While the pace of change varies among different occupations and industries, according to their competitive pressures and the ease of computability, the effect is the same. The routine is bled away, leaving nothing but the exceptional aspects of the job.

Technology of every kind produces generally the same result. A better tool, of any description, makes the worker work harder and improves the life of the consumer. Since nothing human-made is free, no advance comes without effort. That there is confusion on this point explains the occupational uncertainty among both the young and the old. When a machine bends a piece of metal and the blacksmith no longer has to bash it into submission, it's easy to conclude that tools make life easier. But that means that the machine has assumed part of the blacksmith's job, and the blacksmith must therefore now direct his attention to more complicated (that is, more difficult) procedures. For a period of time (the length of which depends on the competitive conditions), the blacksmith may be able to let the machine do the work and continue to charge his customers as if it was his. (The accountant who first used the computer did this, for a short time.) But eventually customers and competitors will notice, and the blacksmith (and the accountant) must now do more complicated work or withdraw.

This process actually produces two categories of jobs. The blacksmith's work becomes more demanding, but there is now the new job of "machine tender." These people end up with the most simplistic, highly repetitious jobs. In other words, the technology has broken the job into two parts, giving all the challenge of greater complexity to one worker and leaving the remains — the stripped-down job — to another. However, those who tend the machines are, by definition, merely waiting to be replaced. The simple nature of their work usually invites yet another technological advance. The effect of this is often disguised, since our workplaces continue to employ those whose work is very straightforward. There are those who merely "pick and package," or who stand at a cash register and take money. We don't often think of the large number of low-skilled jobs that would exist if technology had not already taken over so many functions. Without barcode readers, for example, armies of additional sales clerks would have been necessary. And unmanned barcode readers/cash registers are only a few years from widespread adoption.

Computing produces the same effect, an effect that reaches its apex with expert systems. Originally, the harder work the blacksmith was forced to perform involved more complex steps that needed more knowledge, but it was still repetitious. Nevertheless, he needed to master more complicated steps to accomplish a more difficult task, and this mastery required progressively more education, training, and experience. We can see this same progression at work in other fields too. The master tool and die maker is skilled in the same sense as the university-trained engineer, historian, teacher, or physician. Of course, professionals tend to think of themselves and their education as qualitatively different from that of people in the so-called skilled trades, yet the distinction is pale. They all learn complex steps to solve a problem and then apply them again and again. And over time, they will modify the procedure whenever they learn a new piece of technology, to again be repeated until the next modification. (University education does afford its students more opportunity for curiosity-driven learning and unspecialized problem solving, however. Some students take advantage of these avenues and some do not.)

WHY A CODE MONKEY?

Computing's first effects are similar to those of any technology: work becomes more complex but remains largely repetitious. And the technology brings with it armies of data-entry clerks and machine tenders, like the sales clerks at the computerized point-of-purchase terminals (what were once called cash registers). Computing has also created a surging demand for the old-style skill, one last great manifestation of the traditional job. As the computer industry continues to recruit programmers and developers, they confirm the traditional view of work as no more than a series of complex steps to be repeated; in the case of computing, much of the work is very complicated and very repetitious.

Unfortunately, this is misleading a very large number of people, and these people are now seeking career success based on a model that is about to grow irrelevant. But who can be against this necessary and challenging work, or fail to notice a genuine shortage of these skilled workers and their high salaries? The danger is not what is happening today, but the use of today as a model for the tomorrow that the computer industry itself is creating. One might have thought that the modern world would have taught us not to judge the future by merely trending forward the present.

However, the ongoing advance of computing produces another effect far different from that of previous technologies. Its programmability means that this machine does not just replace repetitious work with more complex repetitious work. Computing (that is, the expert system) is capable of replacing *all* repetitious work. If it is a repeated task, it can be programmed. If it can be programmed, it will be.

It makes no difference to computing whether the task being replaced is that of a welder, stock clerk, engineer, physician, economist, or investment dealer. The repetitious aspects of every job can and will become computer code. The work that is left to humans will therefore become extraordinarily difficult. No longer will it be good enough for workers to repeat complex steps they have memorized; now they will have to produce new steps.

Ironically enough, by providing a huge increase in old-fashioned work to create products that will destroy old-fashioned work, the computer industry confuses itself (or would, if it ever thought about itself). Since much of the work involved in developing and creating software is repetitious, the computer is well able to apply itself to its own products. It will certainly do so to an increasing degree in the future. But the industry is currently distracted by short-term goals and rewards. It often chooses to push products through established pathways instead of trying even a small innovative shortcut. Companies often fear that any delay resulting from experimentation would cause them to lose the market to swifter competitors. Of course, if companies were developing products other than commodity software, they could get off this treadmill.

Nevertheless, expert programming systems will become a powerful specialty. After all, their market is driven by the commodity software's relentless need to develop and upgrade. The continuing rapid growth of computing will still leave room for traditional work for a while yet, if only because of the delay in introducing new work procedures. But the repetitious aspects of software development will be eliminated soon —

sooner than most people think. And many of those who thought their jobs were secure will be unpleasantly surprised by this turn of events. But what applies to computing applies to the rest of the world as well.

As repetition is removed from all work, only the exceptional remains. The exceptional, by definition, is a problem that cannot be solved by any of the known applications of past procedures. If it could have been solved in this way, the computer would have done so. It is difficult to overstate the demands that this exceptional work will make on us, or to exaggerate how unprepared we are to understand the challenge. Exceptional tasks obviously require a creative or innovative response. But what exactly does that mean?

EVER NEWER

Innovations can appear in many forms, although not necessarily as a piece of machinery or a software code. Embodied in anything from a book to a machine, an innovation is intended to offer an improvement in technology that is desirable to the consumer and will be welcomed in the marketplace. The word "innovation" describes the entire process of creating, developing, testing, and moving the improvement into the marketplace, and the scope of this process is often underestimated. When the pieces are treated separately — when, for example, marketing is divorced from research and development — the risk of a failed innovation grows.

The degree of innovation plays a critical role in both the generation of the new idea and its effect. An innovation must be a departure from past practice (or it is not new), but that departure can be slight, radical, or anything in between. All these degrees of innovation are desirable as long as the consumer approves. However, consumers, through the marketplace, are expressing a clear instruction: innovate faster and make the innovations of greater consequence. That is not their explicit preference, of course; they are led by the "invisible hand" of the marketplace to demand the acceleration of human progress, exactly as Adam Smith predicted they would be. As competitive pressures continue to rise, technological innovation (that is, all innovation) becomes one of the few sources of significant competitive advantage. So competition drives companies to increase their attempts at innovation, even as innovation is simultaneously one of the principal sources of rising competition. Successful innovation ratchets up competitive pressures, in other words, and that sets off another wave of attempted innovation. Innovation is therefore driven by a self-sustaining acceleration, a defining characteristic of our age.

The result of this powerful pressure to innovate is that continuous improvement has become the economic norm. Everyone is expected to improve everything all the time. Of course, the most common innovations are those that are the easiest to make, the small departures from past practice. These have now become normal, and because they are normal, they no longer confer competitive advantage. They merely prevent a company from falling behind. To seize a competitive advantage, a company must now produce an innovation that is a significant departure from past practice. And tomorrow the degree of departure will increase yet again. It is the relentless logic of the marketplace, which is always demanding more of everything, including innovation. The trend is utterly clear: most workers are being forced into becoming agents of progressively greater change. Of course, managers will have to be more radical than those they supervise — with the chief executive the most radical of all — or they will not justify their level of responsibility. To say that this requirement is not clearly appreciated is an understatement.

Fortunately, from society's point of view, the accelerating demand for innovation is occurring exactly as the need for non-innovative work is falling. In other words, the supply of workers available to shift from repetitious work to creative work is rising. In a fundamental sense, the market is doing what it is supposed to do: encouraging the reallocation of resources from where they are not wanted to where they are. But how many of those workers are going to be both willing and able to so dramatically reorient their worklife? And how long will it take them to make this change?

Sharp or radical change can take many forms. An existing process can be extended to a new application (using ASA to treat a heart attack, for example, instead of a headache). Or an existing process or product can be made much cheaper (the Internet as a communication facility, for example). Extending a process to an application far outside the normal scope of the technology can also be a significant innovation (such as advances in rocketry applied to car design), as can replacing part of a process with a new one (laser printing instead of photocopying). To replace the entire methodological assumptions of an existing technology is clearly radical change (as will happen when expert systems replace commodity software).

MYTH OF GENIUS

Although small innovations are commonplace, organizations are struggling with the need to create those of greater degree. This is particularly true in the computing industry. But the entire innovation process is poorly appreciated, even though research has identified key features and documented many of the characteristics of successful innovators. Unfortunately, it has proven very difficult to use this information to produce innovation dependably. In fact, many large organizations fail to create a single significantly successful innovation over the course of many years and many attempts. Perhaps there is an essential ingredient we do not yet understand, or perhaps our understanding is adequate but there are organizational obstacles to the implementation of many innovations.

The lack of sustained success by many companies gives rise to the great excuse that afflicts all creative endeavour. This view holds that true innovation is unpredictable, the product of an exceptional and somewhat strange mind. Therefore, since neither event nor person can be part of a planned process, there is no reason to try. A standard R&D operation will take care of small, evolutionary innovations, and the rest is luck.

Logically, this attitude is inconsistent with the intensity of focus that is needed to encourage one of the most difficult of human tasks. But it is easy to see how, without quick results, even a well-considered program to encourage innovation can fall prey to such an attitude, and be abandoned in all but name. Unfortunately, the continued existence of the program adds to the belief that even with time, it is nearly impossible to predict (i.e., plan for) innovation.

Innovation also asks corporations to exhibit two qualities that are notoriously in short supply: patience and the acceptance of failure. Yet both are absolutely vital for successful innovation, as has long been understood. Demanding tasks, by definition, take a long time to accomplish; innovation takes so long precisely because it is so difficult. An innovation, it must be remembered, involves going beyond the learned lessons of the past; innovators must consider a new range of new possibilities. That range is enormous, virtually unlimited. Since it takes time to absorb and evaluate even a small selection of the possibilities, innovation without patience is pure luck. You find your new technique or product within the first one hundred tries or you give up. But all too often, success waited for you at attempt 7,913.

Also, any significant innovation is an experiment (if it wasn't, it wouldn't be a departure from past practice). Any experiment can potentially fail, of course, and by all the laws of probability, some are *guaranteed* to fail. Unless an organization can accept failure as an inevitable consequence of experimentation, innovation cannot occur. Large public corporations are often so driven by short-term earnings reports that both patience and failure are anathema to them. Investors are, of course, ultimately responsible for this quandary. Innovation is great, their behaviour implies, so long as it does not come with a cost. It is no happy sight to see investors trying to violate the most basic laws of economics. We need only ask the dot-com investors.

Smaller companies, on the other hand, often do not have the resources to wait for patience to be rewarded, and one big failure can destroy them. Here investors must also bear some responsibility for starving innovation, even while they claim that innovative products are the very reason they support smaller companies in the first place. Often, of course, they care more about the possibilities of the quick flip than they do about the technological innovation itself. The result is that many smaller companies fail, and the few that do create new products have sometimes simply been lucky enough to hit on the right idea quickly. For both large and small companies, luck does play a large role in the generation of successful innovation, giving support to the idea of unpredictability. In fact, luck is all you can have when an organized program for innovation is absent.

Computer companies are no exception. The typical frenzied rush to market of many software companies reflects their utter lack of patience and aversion to experimental error. These conditions guarantee that any innovations that are created will be no more than safe, evolutionary improvements, and such small improvements can only rarely alter the commodity aspect of most of these products. The prevalence of commodity software (that is, software with no proprietary distinction) is not surprising, since most computer companies do not try to do more. Of the thousands of development companies, only a few are lucky enough to hit the motherlode. Yet the industry makes a virtue of this, celebrating a fire-at-anything-on-the-spur-of-the-moment approach. In the rush to develop a new piece of software that they hope will be an overnight sensation, these companies rarely do market research. They merely lurch from one trendy imitative idea to the next, trusting that if they try enough of them in rapid sequence, one will strike home. Of course, they can do that only until the money runs out. But this approach is so strongly ingrained in everyone, including investors, that failed developers can sometimes reorganize and start again with new money. Unfortunately, while these second attempts are common enough, they are often not that much more thoughtful. Larger computer companies sometimes adopt a more coherent approach, but because of the pressure to maintain market share, they have limits to their patience and their aversion to failure remains acute.

METHOD INSTEAD OF MADNESS

The obstacles to innovation in all industries might seem insurmountable, if not for two circumstances. First, what the market wants, the market gets — sooner or later. And second, the later it gets it, the more powerful the reward. Market opportunities will eventually push either an existing player or a new entrant to break out of its conventional rut and provide the radical changes the market demands. As its powerful lead investor, Bill Gates could have asked Microsoft to take the time and bear the risk of creating a disruptive new technology. Though he was reluctant to do this in the past, Gates now describes Microsoft's .Net initiative as just such a move. The company does seem prepared to let this array of Web-mounted products slowly evolve into prominence. (Of course, patience is a necessary but not sufficient condition for break-through success.)

As the pioneers demonstrate that their more patient approach works, others will find that their investors expect them to follow. The profusion of new and proprietary products, including expert systems, will cause considerable market disruption; market shares are likely to vary widely as existing players and new entrants struggle over many categories of new products.

The second factor that will facilitate the creation of radical innovation is the advent of expert systems for innovation. These systems will not replace the need for patience or an acceptance of failure — after all, no piece of software is ever going to repeal the laws of science — but they will speed the process enough that eternal patience will no longer be necessary. These systems will also reduce the risk of failure and its consequent cost. Overall, they will make the process of radical innovation much more practical by dismissing pure luck and leaving only calculated probability.

Such an expert program will repudiate the belief that innovation is mysterious by pacing the user through each of its many steps. Taking the form of a suite of programs, innovation systems begin by delivering the data that maximizes the likelihood of innovative insight. Empty brains are not creative brains, no matter how often "information" is decreed to be an obstacle to creativity. (This erroneous belief explains much about the state of the "artistic" and entertainment worlds.)

It is true that a knowledge of how past problems were solved can implicitly and inappropriately narrow the focus of your search for improved solutions; you will always be tempted to tweak rather than to transform. For those who have actually employed the past solutions, the temptation is all the more powerful. But to free yourself from the constraint of convention by ignoring it is to commit the ultimate anti-intellectual act. It is to guarantee that your future work will duplicate both the mistakes and the accomplishments of the past, except for those rare occasions when you stumble on a new insight — assuming, of course, that you are not so ignorant that you fail to see the significance of what you have tripped over.

However, you can minimize the tunnel-vision effect of information by selecting that information with care. The expert information tools described earlier in this book already begin to address this issue. By removing false and misleading information, and therefore steering you away from blind alleys, they help speed the process of innovation. They are also designed to facilitate broader, more multidisciplinary enquiries, and to identify emerging areas of discussion. Taken together, they offer a rich and diversified fund of information, providing more fertile terrain for your imagination than the dusty ground of short-term technical data.

Creativity originates from a panoply of information, information that differs in discipline, scope, domain, methodology, source, consequence, culture, history, and certainty. The worker is only as good as his or her materials, however, in this as in every other endeavour. And while existing information tools make a positive contribution to innovation, they are less effective than they could be. The expert system would recast these products to maximize their diversity and scope. A survey interface that would allow workers to view information in a way that captures both its diversity and its interconnections would be especially important. Unfortunately, information overload rears its ugly head yet again, and this survey would itself have to be a creative expression, almost surely driven by the interesting mathematics that tries to organize infinite sets of numbers. It must, of course, be flexible enough that its configuration cannot prejudice human thought. (Actually, it would have to be infinitely flexible, to make sure that would never happen.) In an overall sense, creation software becomes the apex of software, drawing on almost all other software facilities.

FIRE IN THE BELLY

Besides marshalling information, innovation software will help to define the interests of researchers. The need to be imaginative and practical at the same time so presses human capability that, in the absence of an intense interest in the domain in question, it becomes almost impossibly difficult. It is reasonable to ask professional workers to make an *evolutionary* change in their area of expertise. It is not reasonable to ask them to create a breakthrough innovation, however, unless they have an independent and powerful interest in the issue at hand. Ideally, passion is the prerequisite.

This fact alone explains why evolutionary changes are quite common and blockbuster ideas are not. It is why all younger people must be told to nurture their strongest interests. Without passion, they will not be able to rise beyond the level of pedestrian improvement, even as the marketplace demands a response beyond that.

Any organization that is truly committed to major innovation has no choice but to recruit and allocate its lead innovators based on intense interest. (The phrase "intense interest" will be used because "passion" sounds unbusinesslike to many.) The old rule used to be that experience fundamentally implies interest, but this is not necessarily true to even the most casual observer of business. And education is certainly not a dependable indicator of interest, as any professor well knows. But identifying interest is not an easy matter. Many people do not know what their real interests are and have never considered the matter in any organized way. They end up being "interested" in whatever falls their way — in life as much as in work. Others will convincingly lie about their interests, or sometimes the lack thereof. We need a tool to help individuals explore their strengths of interest, and to confirm that strength to third parties. The issue is complicated by the fact that interests also change and evolve, however; defining them in these circumstances is like searching for an ever-shifting target.

PLUGGED INTO THE MARKET

Effective innovation must address the customer's wants and goals. This connection is often overlooked, even when the innovation is modest and the market research more easily done. Moreover, market research in its traditional sense runs into trouble when faced with sharp departures from past practice. The sharper the departure, the fewer the "signposts" that can be smoothly extended into the future. It is difficult to estimate the demand for a product that never existed before. It is even difficult to gauge the consumer's concern about a problem for which a radical new solution is being proposed (because consumers give little thought to problems for which there appear to be no solutions). Hence, the innovator is often told that there is no market for the new product because the customer does not think there is a problem to be solved. Still, it needs to be emphasized that making customers aware that there is now a solution will not immediately cause them to appreciate the problem. This is a long process of education and intellectual thought; the more radical the idea, the longer the process.

Unfortunately, innovators often respond to this challenge by trusting their instincts and developing their product. Then they try to break through the customer's barrier of inertia, hoping that the money does not run out before the barrier falls. Often, the money *does* run out. But often, too, the innovators should not have trusted their instincts in the first place. If the product does not meet the customer's need at an affordable price, it will not sell, no matter how aggressively the pitch is made.

There is, therefore, a need for an expert briefing program, which would sensitize innovators to society's needs. This search engine would be very carefully calibrated to identify underlying "themes" in human activity. It would select and match data from the widest range of sources and types, and shape that data into a vision of the future. For example, a properly constituted briefing program would suggest that family relationships are growing strongly in importance, and that this trend shows every sign of continuing far into the future. The software would paint an image, drawing on quantitative measurements of the attention paid to family issues in the news media, popular culture, scholarly literature, and advertising. It would also consider demographic trends, consumer spending patterns, personal investment trends, and so on. Massaging all these diverse data into a coherent view is an interesting computer problem. While innovators can already produce roughly the same briefing effect by reading many books, the software would offer a much more efficient and comprehensive survey of divergent strains of thought.

This software would be prized because the information it created could be of great commercial significance. We already know the growing importance of family relationships dramatically affects many types of product innovations and marketing campaigns. Disney runs ads suggesting that parents take the children to its theme park so that they have memories to share when the children grow older and no longer want to take family vacations. It also uses separate ads to encourage couples with grown children to go there alone (one includes a "sad" grown child for comic effect). But the better ad would encourage grown children and their parents to go to the park together — that is, it would encourage multi-generational vacations. Such holidays are, in fact, growing in popularity. An alert tourist operator would tailor and market its services for the whole family — grandparents, grown children, and grandchildren.

The expert briefing software would also address a serious contradiction that exists between two of the preconditions for successful innovation: the importance of the innovator's preferences, and the need to satisfy the wants and goals of others. Some curiosity-driven researchers, especially those at universities, take the extreme position that they need pay attention only to their own interests, since no one knows how any discovery might be used. But while discoveries *might* be used in any number of truly unpredictable ways, it is not the case that *all* aspects of a potential discovery are uncertain.

For innovators supported by public funds, the answer is not to ask them to put aside their personal passions, since that limits any kind of innovation; rather, they must be asked to be sensitive to society's needs, and to consider how their interests might address the most important of these needs. It is difficult to see why responsible people would choose to act in any other way, unless they were so ignorant of society that they did not know how to make such a choice. Eventually, society's public agencies will require this response, rather than the vague or confused homilies of the present. Of course, a professional researcher who has no strong interests can be given detailed directions without any adverse consequences; the lazy have a tendency to cloak themselves in "interest" to avoid such instructions.

In the corporate context, the employer has an obvious right to provide more direction, and it is, therefore, to his or her advantage to select employees for their pre-existing interest in the subject at hand. Nevertheless, for both the company and its innovators, the briefing software accommodates the organization's competency and interests. It invites the worker to see where his or her interests and capabilities can be of the most use to the organization. Any person who cannot see how this software could exactly be used has missed the basic logic: this software is not *exact* in any way, nor is it intended to be.

THE ELITE TUTOR

While the software tools discussed above can all contribute to successful innovation, there is a core function that, if missing, renders the entire process questionable. Without imagination, all the preparatory steps are in vain. Even if you have a rich background of information, passionate interest, and sensitivity to the consumer's problem, you must still be able to generate new possibilities to see what could be done. You must be able to take any problem or piece of knowledge and rotate it through time and space, looking at it in many different ways. How many ways? As many as it takes until you find the answer you seek. In the world of imagination, there is no limit to the number of ways something can be seen or done. Hence, the human mind touches the infinite in the most operational sense, although this is very difficult for most people to do. Young children appear to have much less difficulty, although their undeveloped range of expression constrains their creative impulses.

It is no surprise at all that most adults struggle with imaginative skill. After the brief Shangri-La of childhood, most adults put aside daydreaming and stolidly march forward. The school system reinforces this tendency, when it is not positively punishing creativity. The conventions and rules of society further ingrain habit of thought. And the sheer difficulty of imagining something that could come true is the final discouragement. Some people simply cannot conjure up any imaginative vision, whether realizable or not. This inadequacy is then excused with the unfounded assertion that creativity is the preserve of a few rare persons.

Of course most adults have trouble being creative. How anyone could expect to be adept at imagination without ever having practised it is impossible to understand, especially in a world where everyone knows that practice is needed to hit a little ball with a big stick. There is an overwhelming and unappreciated need for an expert tutorial program for imagination. But while such software would shape the practice to make it as effective and efficient as possible, it will not work overnight. It will serve only the dedicated user or an insightful employer.

The program would be elegantly simple: it would ask a question that required a machine-processable yet imaginative response. (The response would have to be constrained, however, since it is too easy to give a non-sensical creative answer.) The program would compare the response to its memory of established practices, rejecting any answer that matched the memory. The user would then answer the same question again, until he or she produced a response that no longer duplicated an established idea. For example, the program could ask for a plot synopsis not duplicated in a database of thousands of plots. It could ask for a joke for a given situation and compare it to the largest published collections of such material. It could ask for the design of a city centre that did not match something already recorded in an atlas of all the world's major urban areas.

The program would have the capacity to deal with either an exact duplication or a close imitation. The beginning user would be allowed a few close imitations. Fortunately, many of the established answers are available in electronic form (or can be translated from non-digital form). A particularly aggressive level of the program would require answers that could not be found on the Internet or in a full-text general-use database. The program would proceed through advancing levels as the user grew more proficient, asking questions on greatly varied topics.

Those who doubt the need for such a system should note that most people have difficulty conjuring up even a modest sexual fantasy, despite a powerful incentive. Whips, chains, and leather underwear can hardly be considered imaginative, and the program's request for a sexual fantasy not duplicated in the world's erotic literature will constitute a very difficult challenge. There are also aspects of this program that could be entertaining in a game-like format, since this is, after all, the basic game question turned on its head: find what is not there. But the core function of this program is a relentless and rigorous regime of practice. And so it must be. Imagination is an unbounded domain, and the practice must reflect this.

The above description of the tutorial program is of course crude, and is intended only as an illustration of what could be done. The actual system would require extensive research, a precisely planned structure, and meticulous care. But none of its features would have to advance beyond conventional research or computing.

Since routine work will fade under the pressure of expert systems, the need to reorient workers becomes a matter of the highest social and economic priority. It is, therefore, the height of irony that expert systems will help in that reorientation — directly spurring the ability of each and every worker to do something new.

CHAPTER TEN

EDUCATION: FOUNTAINHEAD OF THE INFORMATION INDUSTRIES

NOBLE OR PROFITABLE?

Education, in both its public and private forms, is one of the great enterprises of humanity, and it is destined to grow in relative and absolute terms. Expert systems will play a central role in this growth, even as education fuels the capability of these systems. Libraries and their expert access systems provide the grist for the mill for all students. Research, the product of an educated mind, makes expert software possible; yet without this software, many kinds of research are impossible. Expert systems and education are inextricably linked in society and in the marketplace, and those who seek commercial advantage in computing will have to recognize that in almost every computer application, an educational aspect lurks. But confusion about this relationship is widespread.

The scope of this opportunity cannot be recognized unless education is seen in its broadest sense. Expert systems both affect and are affected by every type of educational endeavour, from kindergarten classes to doctoral programs, from public education to private training, from weekend seminars to global consulting practices. All educators are engaged in packaging and disseminating learning. But some, such as university researchers, consultants, and expert developers, are also creators of new learning. Expert systems will have a symbiotic relationship with these people — both selling them their products and drawing on them for talent and the expertise that is at the heart of these products. Expert systems will leave no educational practice or mission unchanged, and the march into education will be driven by the power of profit.

Education is surely a noble calling, and nobility does move resources, albeit slowly and painfully. Schools are started as community-minded endeavours, and yet they can just as easily suffer from community neglect. The haunting call of pure profit is still the fastest way to move mountains of resources. Unfortunately, in this imperfect world, educational expert systems will thrive exactly because they make profit. And they make profit because they help other players make profit. It is no more complicated than that.

Leaders of business, although they may recognize the societal value of education, have no choice but to acknowledge that without educated workers, they will be reduced to fighting over the table scraps left by their better-educated competitors. Educated skill is now the prerequisite for successful enterprise. That fact alone is a harbinger of future social and economic success. Schools are now too important to be left to the teachers, too important for the rhetorical musing of politicians. Education is integral to business, and that will thrust expert systems into what were once the most sacrosanct of educational precincts.

The disjointed and chaotic arguments surrounding education are indicative of the undeveloped state of this art. But there are several clear observations that can be made. Public universal education — and to a lesser extent, private education — has had a net positive effect on society. To deny this is to reject the evidence of the past hundred years. We have, for example, created a more literate society (and the fact that it is not as literate as it could be does not change the accomplishment of the past). Overall, we have a more knowledgeable and skilled society now than we had a century ago. The exponential increase in average productivity is the most tangible sign of the effect of education.

It is well understood that this increase in productivity has not just been a result of our having better tools. To a large degree, those tools are useless in the hands of an illiterate and unschooled worker. But education for the masses must be considered a new idea when viewed in any historical context, and therefore some uncertainty over its direction is not surprising. It is a new institution trying to decide what it should do and how it should do it. So education advances and retreats in fits and starts, seemingly almost as confused as the society of which it is a part. But education is so intimately related to the whole range of human experience that to solve education is to "solve" a large share of human despair and distress. It is hard to understand how anyone could think it would be easy.

FORWARD WITHOUT FOCUS

Part of the difficulty is that education is not sure of its own goals. We want students to be literate and numerate; general problem-solvers; flexible; articulate and creative; knowledgeable about history, government, science, technology, the environment, business, and current events. We want them to be concerned citizens and effective parents, to have pride in themselves and in their work; we want them to fight against injustice and have marketable job skills. That short list of goals is, of course, no list at all. It is merely a wish list for better humans, and without being prioritized, it has no operational value. How these priorities are to be set remains in dispute.

Even if it is clear that greater literacy is a high priority, there is no consensus of opinion on how it should be defined or measured. Literacy could include the comprehension of newspapers, workplace instructions, technical texts, classic literature, or the popular vernacular. A single score on a simple test certainly is not how it should be evaluated.

Numeracy is even harder to define and measure. Should it be measured in terms of simple problems or real-world applications? What level of mathematical skill is appropriate? There is, for example, very little evidence available to tell us how many students should be able to do calculus, and no evidence at all to support the proposition that more mathematics is always better. Curriculum development has been hampered by this inability to confirm the validity of much admirable experimentation. Indeed, the difficulties have traditionally been so great that educational researchers have often not bothered to offer more than cursory or anecdotal evidence. As a result, curriculum development has lacked both the discipline and the credibility of the scientific method.

But lest we be tempted to give up, it is vital to note that in every subject area, at every level of education, there are teachers who nurture the love of learning, and who inform, engage, provoke, and inspire their students. Unfortunately, this does not appear to be the norm. But whatever is done once is not impossible. The deficiencies of education are not surprising in our primitive society, although that truth does not excuse either teacher or student. The challenge is to determine what education could be, and to move there with all urgent dispatch. The new ingredient is the expert system, a tool that can advance education in many ways, thus also stimulating other commercial aspects of the information age.

WICKED TESTING

The transformation of education begins with expert systems defining what needs to be taught by providing evaluations of human capability. What you cannot define, you cannot measure; what you cannot measure, you cannot teach. The evaluation will take several forms, yet each will still benefit from patience and memory. Evaluation is inherently boring to the examiner and stressful for the test-taker. With the computer under the control of its expert program, both of these problems are more easily addressed.

The evaluation programs, like all expert software, will require both research and experimentation. Even though these programs will measure talent in all its diverse forms, they will begin with those most commercially attractive. Logic would seem to dictate that these programs would first test the capability of senior management, since incompetence there has such widespread and drastic consequences. However, power relationships will ensure that it is used there last. But when evaluation programs enter the organization, they will inevitably advance upwards.

The first to be tested will be junior staff in finance, marketing, and product development. Each of these fields demands multi-faceted capabilities, which makes them perfect candidates for the computer's methodical probing. Naturally, the test will not be time-limited, nor will it be restricted to a single attempt. The goal is to measure competence, not performance anxiety. The purpose of the research is to make sure these tests avoid the many errors of the past. As a result, they will not concentrate on technical issues, on pure issues of knowledge. They will certainly not bother to test memory (all aids will be permitted), and instead will concentrate on the candidate's research abilities and his or her skill at applying knowledge to a problem. They will also attempt to measure commitment, passion, and integrity.

Most examinations produce poor results today because they are too short and too simplistic to capture quality data. But short, simple tests are all that most organizations, both public and private, educational or not, can afford using the old methods. The computer's low cost and high speed, however, make long, complex tests feasible. Students will be overjoyed at the prospect.

The evaluation program will both generate tasks and "mark" responses. Rather than just drawing on a bank of prepared questions or problems, it must set tasks based on the previous responses of the student. Step by step, patiently and relentlessly, the software will measure the applicant. Managers who see themselves in high-pressure, high-energy environments will be early adopters of these programs, which they will view as perfect for measuring the talents of their junior employees. They will be surprised to discover that they soon end up taking such tests themselves.

Designing the process that will generate the tasks will be the challenge. And as society's needs change, the design will have to respond. The tasks have to be realistic, varied, and compressed enough to push the applicant to his or her limit. These programs will take days, and sometimes weeks, to administer. Those who believe that this would be an unrealistic commitment of time and energy are merely reflecting today's conventional wisdom, which does not treat talent seriously. But the market will destroy those who hold such views.

The tasks the computer sets will always have an unexpected element, which is an essential part of mimicking reality. Such a feature is relatively easy to program, and the test candidate's failure to respond well will be reasonably easy to detect. The task will disguise its fields of inquiry, and the candidate will have to decide which principles are appropriate. For example, a task that asked for a recommended approach to cloning would logically require the candidate to delve into aspects of politics, economics, business, and science. Since it will be a "real" task, the principles will have to be drawn from several different disciplines. The candidate will also have to search for information and offer at least an element of experimental design. At this level, the program will be looking not for a right answer, but for a credible answer. The most important factor will be the candidate's ability to proceed. As the program advances the degree of difficulty, the tasks become more obscure and the relevant principles greater and more varied. The experimental feature will turn into a fully fledged research project. The program will also attempt to select tasks that are related to actual job requirements, so that the evaluation process can serve as genuine preparation for future work. Nevertheless, this preparatory aspect will still be subservient to the evaluation goal.

To detect the candidate's underlying love of learning and scientific rigour, the program will conduct a "mythology" test, which will ask the candidate to identify facts that are popularly held to be true but are in fact false. This feature alone has tremendous commercial appeal. Candidates will be unable to prepare for evaluation, and will fail unless they are educated, experienced, and alert.

The sceptics will again claim that such an evaluation system is impossible without advances in computing technology. But it is not clear, at either a conceptual or a practical level, why the tasks described cannot be expressed in computable form. There is no reason to doubt that excellent digital simulations can be created for many kinds of tasks. That such "exam tasks" do not presently exist is merely evidence that examiners have always been constrained (until now) by the length of the exam and the burden of its interpretation. With the expert system examiner, the test process can be lengthy and still affordable. Experimentation itself now becomes practical.

To still say that this is an unrealistic approach is to deny that sophisticated computerized test simulations already exist. A flight simulator is such an expert system, and it is an indispensable training and evaluation tool. A pilot who routinely crashes the simulator is hardly a pilot anyone would be tempted to hire.

If we can already simulate bringing down a heavily loaded Boeing 747 in a snowstorm with one engine on fire, there is no reason to suppose we cannot simulate a marketing campaign for a new product introduction. Since expert software can already simulate an aircraft making a mid-course correction, there is no reason it cannot simulate a marketplace change of direction. If a pilot can simulate the "soft landing" of a malfunctioning plane, why can't a CEO simulate bringing his or her organization in for a soft landing among economic turbulence? In the real world, we seem content to wait for the CEO to crash into actual, instead of simulated, bankruptcy.

TO MEASURE IS TO MANDATE

The effect of credible tests for important human capabilities should not be underestimated. As long as no such tests exist or are used, actual job performance will be erratic; educational attainment is equally hit and miss. The evaluation programs will provide feedback that will be progressively more difficult to ignore. Many people will face the evaluations and unfortunately deliver an imitation of the work they are supposed to perform. But the indirect evidence suggests that if you hired only those who succeeded in the evaluation, you would be faced with a dire shortage of workers. The solution is clear: those whose present capabilities are inadequate must return for more (and better) education. And the second time around, society and corporate shareholders will expect better results.

Eventually, the evaluation programs will become a continuous part of all educational endeavour, in public institutions and corporate in-house training. This, in turn, will have a profound effect on curriculum. Because the evaluation programs measure actual task performance, artificial subject boundaries are inevitably eroded (because most problems of significance cross boundaries). There will be no evaluation advantage to memorizing information when the only questions the candidate will be asked are those to which the answers could not have been memorized. Teachers will find these changes especially stressful, as the old model will fade faster than they expect.

The effect on corporate training will be equally disruptive. Most seminars, short courses, conferences, and "challenge" experiences will be found to be delivering much less than was promised. Task orientation will sweep aside the quick fixes, buzzwords, pep talks, and disjointed scraps of information that often plague corporations. And productivity will increase as soon as these distractions have been eliminated. Real education, with continuous evaluation, will become the norm as companies take on more and more responsibility for nurturing their employees' capabilities. Those that fail to do so will fail in the marketplace. But strong competitive advantage is waiting for the educational providers that meet the new standards and the companies that respond quickly. At the centre of this transformation will be the expert evaluation programs and their creators.

A REALLY LEVEL PLAYING FIELD

These programs will have a further impact on the job applicant, whether that applicant is a recent graduate or an experienced worker. The young fear, quite correctly, that companies often put little effort into hiring, with the result that hiring decisions are all too often based on inappropriate considerations, back-channel access, or random caprice. Because the young cannot offer confirmed experience, they see themselves as dancing to someone else's tune, trapped in a process over which they have little control.

The experienced often feel they have no more control. It seems to them that some kinds of experience are dismissed casually, especially if the candidate is "too" experienced, too old, or too set in the world of fifteen minutes ago. They suspect that glib new answers have often replaced the older ones, which take more effort.

Both these groups of job applicants now have a tool at their disposal to redress part of the balance. But what can they do about employers and educational institutions that are slow to adopt evaluation programs? It is logical to expect that these programs will be offered at independent test centres, where the young and the experienced will be able to obtain documentation of their capabilities as a challenge to prospective employers. The applicants who fail may recognize the inadequacy of their education or experience, and so be led to seek out the training they need, presumably at a facility that does use the evaluation programs.

THE MOST PATIENT TEACHER

These evaluation programs will naturally encourage the second major category of educational software: the great tutorial programs. No, computers will not replace teachers. However, even though expert programs cannot perform all aspects of education, the ones that they do perform will force change and advancement in other areas. The computer will draw on what is its basic strength: a vast and dependable memory. In effect, it can exhibit patience beyond what any person is capable of. The only challenge for the developer is to find ways to apply that patience to exactly the right aspects of education. To some degree, tutorial programs, such as early reading programs for children, are already available. There are also specialized programs for subject areas from history to surgery. Programs like these will continue to be developed rapidly under the pressure of a marketplace that asks more and more of human performance. The proliferation of these teaching programs is both a problem and an opportunity.

It is essential to evaluate the effectiveness of these tutorial programs rigorously. They cannot simply engage interest (although they must do that) and *appear* to address the skills in question. The tutorial programs must be used in combination with the evaluation programs to ensure maximum effectiveness. One suspects that if the present tutorial programs were evaluated carefully, the variation in quality would be wide. Indeed, the absence of expert evaluation programs slows the development of the tutor. Unless the effectiveness of the tutor can be reliably evaluated, it cannot be improved.

There is another generation of tutorial programs yet to be created, and these programs will be much more powerful and pervasive than those now available. They will, in effect, be companions to the evaluation programs. The tutorial programs of today fall short because they rest on that great inconvenience of education: the need for practice. The more sophisticated the task, the greater the need for practice, and since only sophisticated tasks offer future employment, the need for practice grows rapidly. That is why experience is so valued, except that it is usually "poor practice." It occurs only in an operational environment, where mistakes are either missed or punished and explanation for a failure is rarely communicated. Also, actual workplace tasks are rarely sequenced to walk a person through increasing levels of challenge. Learning takes place only when you have time to think — a luxury that's absent from many workplaces. Experience can of course improve the capability of any worker, but only when it is disciplined by evaluation.

The hard truth is that practice cannot be replaced in either a school system or a corporate environment. Beyond some initial and simple efficiencies, learning cannot be hurried. And the more there is to learn, the more time it will take. Yet if the required amount of practice was to be provided by human tutors, the expense would make it impractical. Human patience is also no rival for that of the computer. Hence the great tutorial programs will provide practice in task accomplishment, from simple tasks to complex ones in a carefully orchestrated sequence. Whenever the worker fails to proceed, the tutor will suggest avenues for improvement and alternative guidance. The tutorial program will have to meet all the criteria of the evaluation program, and then add a large array of open-ended possibilities. These programs will certainly be worth their premium pricing. The tutor will, of course, try to provide exactly as much practice as any individual needs. For many people, the practice period will be long indeed, society's price for satisfying its demand for skilled labour.

THE REAL TEACHER

Human teachers remain as essential as ever. While the tutorial programs use exquisite patience to pace students, human teachers respond to all the exceptions, anomalies, peculiarities, and failures of the tutors. Because the tutors are using real tasks, there will always be exceptions and unusual student responses requiring human attention. If the program did not produce that result, it could only be because the task specification was improperly done. In such a case, the teachers will use their cumulative experience to reset and redesign the tutors.

The tutors will not replace teachers in their other traditional roles: to encourage, to stimulate, to provoke, to engage, to draw out, to inspire, to console, and to serve as a role model. This is the teacher, at any level of accomplishment, doing what the tutorial program can never do. Of course, teachers who can do only the routine part of their job will find the tutor breathing down their necks. The attitudes that the good teacher tries to inculcate are those that the marketplace will demand to an ever greater degree. The tutorial programs, therefore, serve students both by providing better practice tasks than a teacher ever could and by freeing teachers to perform their most critical functions.

As the evaluation and tutorial programs gain acceptance, they explicitly demand content and task specification. Eventually, it will occur to someone to *determine* what minimum content everyone needs to know, and what tasks represent society's highest priorities. Those who wish to answer those questions with assurance have a variety of research tools at their disposal. Using information technologies, it is possible to identify the more used pieces of basic information. Indeed, with careful queries, you could identify the most commonly used fact on any topic. Similarly, it is possible to identify key task categories by frequency of use, by links to other tasks, and by prerequisite of use. There is simply no need to guess about these matters. Some of the content now usually included in educational curricula will be revealed to be of peripheral use, while other content will need to be reinforced. Priority tasks will cross traditional disciplines, emphasizing research, integration, interpretation, and innovation.

Even young children must be asked to conduct investigations that require them to consult more than one source, to make empirical observations, to undertake limited experiments, and to report on their findings. As the students progress into post-secondary schooling, they must perform the above tasks more aggressively. Finally, the student must attempt explicit innovations, which will be evaluated only on process and not on outcome. Since communication skills will have to claim a dramatically greater share of the curricular weight, research will need to reveal what content can be reduced.

SCHOOL AS FACTORY?

There will be some who view these educational trends as highly objectionable. They will claim that the new schooling is removing the human factor when it is actually strengthening it. The evaluation tests will be depicted as highly stressful, and therefore will be seen to promote student anxiety and consequent failure. But that danger merely emphasizes the teacher's duty to encourage and support. The tutorial programs will be denounced as a harsh, relentlessly demanding regime of study. Actually, that is the demand of the marketplace, not the tutorial programs. Here, again, the teacher will have to nurture determination, conviction, persistence, and discipline, while never once discounting the capability of the student.

Opponents will claim that the end result is a rigid, prescriptive, and narrow focus — bastardized education for the corporate elite. But by focusing on task, the tutorial program accommodates any learning style and sees as much value in art as it does in physics. Instead of serving a narrow constituency, it strives to teach effectiveness and create talent for use in the domain of the individual's choosing. The confused and the baffled, the ignorant and the apathetic, the disorganized and the unfocused, the careless and the undisciplined — all these people are always and everywhere at the mercy of the powerful. Educational software will move to redress part of the balance.

Unfortunately, the controversy will be heightened by the fact that some educational programs will promise much and deliver little. A few, by encouraging narrowly inflexible approaches and misdirecting the student's attention, will be positively dangerous. Part of this will be the unavoidable junk that gets created in any expanding field.

THE PROFESSOR AND THE EXPERT SYSTEM

Expert educational software will have a great and beneficial impact on education at all levels, although the transition period will be costly and disruptive. The effect will be stronger the higher the level of education. With young children and disadvantaged adults, the human factor must be maintained to a greater degree. The suggestion that children will largely learn at home on the Net is absurd, and adults will do so only in particular applications. Education, we must remind ourselves repeatedly in a society that forgets, is not the mastery of facts or even of procedure — it teaches students how to accomplish tasks that are valued by society. Education minus social interaction, which does not occur on the Internet, is like preparing to do battle in a closet.

At more advanced educational levels, however, the age and experience of the students facilitates independent work in front of a screen, and thus much of the present work of teachers is stripped away. They still have responsibilities, but the demands on them will change sharply. The teacher who cannot encourage or nurture is irrelevant. The teacher whose own command of knowledge is barely adequate is equally irrelevant, because he or she will be unable to respond to student queries, all of which will concern the exceptional and the very difficult. The teacher who lives in the ivory tower will be helpless to address the problem of task accomplishment. These problems will be most pronounced at the universities.

Universities, by long tradition, have had a somewhat vague approach to the quality of education. These are, after all, institutions that do not require their teachers to have any formal education in teaching. The incongruity of that for an educational facility that sees itself at the apex of learning is testimony to the power of tradition over the most elemental logic. Only recently have university administrators thought to make teaching success a prerequisite for promotion and tenure, often using the most primitive of evaluation tools. Yet here more than anywhere, the educational programs will take over a very large part of the work of many professors. The problem is that some professors have a limited understanding of their other teaching roles. Some have no desire at all to perform those roles, and so will celebrate the programs for freeing them from irksome duties. They will then happily retreat to their offices or labs to do the research they truly love. That might be fine, except that the marketplace wants much more from its university graduates and their teachers. And one way or the other, the universities will have no choice but to respond.

Competitive pressures demand that university graduates master the most difficult of tasks, those that go beyond today's standard of accomplishment, that offer a degree of explicit creative response. And tomorrow the degree of creativity will be even higher. However, the tutorial programs can only pace students through the known tasks and responses. The software will ask the student to enter a land of shadows at the edge of human experience and understanding. But the digital tutors will do this knowing that here the professors will intervene, providing that subtle blend of encouragement and guidance that allows both teacher and student to walk forward, with the teacher ensuring that together they do not fall into a pit.

Whether the supply of this level of teaching will be adequate to the rising demand for it is in doubt. Indeed, there can be nothing but doubt when the institutions involved do not give full priority to excellence in teaching (although for many professors, it is a personal priority). An institutional response is required, and from a deeply conservative institution at that. It is difficult to imagine that the universities' adaptation to this new economic reality will be anything other than painful.

The powerful effects of software on universities in particular and on education in general cannot be viewed as surprising. Computing in its most advanced state will have the greatest impact in those fields that are information- or knowledge-intensive, such as consulting, finance, research, and government. But education is the most information-intensive of all, and here the impact will be greatest.

CHAPTER ELEVEN

CONSULTING: MENTOR, SERVANT, AND GUARDIAN ANGEL

EXPERTS BY DEFINITION

While the consulting industry is one of society's educational agents, it does have characteristics and scale that render it distinct enough to warrant separate consideration. In an increasingly complex world, consulting can only grow in importance. Still, it's a relative newcomer to the information sector, and much of its development still lies ahead. The speed with which consulting rises to future challenges will have a powerful effect on both its clients and the computing industry (to which it is inextricably linked).

The consulting industry offers advice in fields that range across accounting, management, engineering, computing, public relations, advertising, marketing, economics, human relations, and many other disciplines. The essential differences among consultancies are reflected in their expertise, but not in the way they do business or win customers. Moreover, as business problems grow more complex and diverse, they are inevitably pulled onto each other's turf. And of course, the computing industry unites them all.

There is hardly a credible consultant who does not use computing as a significant tool. And for many of them, their ability to use this tool gives them a competitive advantage in the delivery of their services. Of course, some consultants provide explicit computing advice to their clients, in addition to providing advice in other areas. It is therefore clear that computing, especially expert systems, will play a pivotal role in shaping tomorrow's consulting industry.

Because it provides answers to complex problems, the expert system is a natural companion to consulting. Since consultants have only expertise to sell, they are often the primary users of the expert systems, almost all of which have direct applicability to the consultants' responsibilities. And because these programs often seem "radical" or difficult to use, consultants will find it necessary (and profitable) to encourage and advise their clients on their operation. In addition, these programs will often induce the kind of organizational stress that invites further advice. A clear initial effect of expert systems will be the stimulation of consulting. Many consultants will notice and respond appropriately.

Expert systems can also be applied to the full range of consulting activities. Some programs, like those for information management, will apply to any business situation, and others, like distribution programs, will be tailored to the consultancy's specific market. As a result, much of the future growth of consulting will be affected by the development of expert systems.

There will, however, be some delay in achieving the full benefits of the synergistic relationship between computing and consulting. The first obstacle involves those consultants who do not see themselves as true information professionals. These people elevate fads to dogma and are too content to lift a scrap of an idea out of the latest book they half read. This, of course, explains the highly uneven quality of consulting, as well as the armies of clients who have been badly disappointed. Unsatisfactory results can also be generated by clients who lust after a magic bullet to solve all their problems; some consultants are only too happy to give it to them — between the eyes.

Thoroughly professional firms will, however, also feel challenged on several fronts by expert systems. While they will quite readily use the programs for their own work, and will be particularly eager to use evaluation software for their own staff, there will be some uneasiness about putting such software in the hands of the clients. There may be a tendency to see the expert programs as competitors. The answer is, of course, for the consultants to push their expertise beyond that of the programs. In doing so, they will redefine their traditional role, expanding beyond the mere dissemination of established knowledge, a mandate all too close to that of the software.

Consultants will also struggle to adjust partly because the basic logic of expert software is less familiar to them than might be expected. While consultants have always accessed information and conducted research of various kinds, they are not used to doing the amount of research necessary for this kind of software. Traditionally, their expertise was adequate to serve most of their clients' needs, and this expertise was based more on experience and education than on original research. But as the world moves on, the consultant's edge begins to erode. Simple problems will be resolved by machines, with only complicated matters remaining. And each year, the complexity barrier separating machines and consultants will rise yet again.

MAKE SOMEONE PAY

Even those consultants who would like to do more aggressive research are limited because they often have few ways to leverage that knowledge into revenue. A single client, even a small group of clients, may not be able to bear the cost. While consultants, both large and small, do try to sell the same observations over and over again, competition among the firms makes this more difficult.

Software, by contrast, offers a different way to sell solutions (that is, information). First, it does not require the consultant's personal contact time, and so it is already more profitable. And because software can be distributed more easily, whether by ASP or not, a greater number of customers can be served. This means that there are now research questions that can be profitably addressed, but only when the answer is delivered by software. The challenge to the consultant is that the new "software" answers supersede their older, less advanced answers.

Given the unenlightened state of our world, it is not particularly surprising that no one wants to bear the cost of finding the answer to a very difficult question. And since the private marketplace is unable to charge for the answer, such research is largely left to the government, acting for society. Unfortunately, the support of the public for research of every kind has typically been low. In a society that does not *generally* love learning, this is hardly surprising. Even research of the most commanding usefulness receives only nickels and dimes. Medical research is the classic underfunded domain, even though it offers life and health. Even business research is more likely to be conducted within university business schools than private corporations. Expert systems begin to moderate this shortage of research support, however, by making it more practical to sell the answers.

Those who decry the commercialization of knowledge entirely miss the point. When something that was untradable becomes tradable, its supply will rise. This is one of the most basic laws of economics. This does not necessarily reduce the role of public authorities in the funding of research, even if it serves as a pretext for that. After all, only some kinds of applied research can be sold as expert systems. Other kinds of applied research, and almost all pure research, still has to be funded by non-commercial agencies (that is, by government and private charities). Even though pure research has no immediate commercial applications, and therefore cannot be supported by private companies, it remains the base from which applied discoveries are made. In an economy that holds innovation as the key engine of advancement, the state will have a continuing obligation to fund pure research, and to do so at increasing levels. It should, of course, quickly download any activities that can be funded by the software companies in their pursuit of expert systems.

THE GRAND MASTERS

Expert programs will put consulting practices under considerable stress as part of their traditional areas of business are lost to them. But this development merely changes consulting, without necessarily even slowing its rate of growth. Consultants will become more like teachers, with whom they already have a lot in common. As routine issues become the province of the software program, consultants will deal only with the exceptions. With each year, the exceptions will become more exceptional, pressing the consultant's expertise. This represents a great challenge because, by definition, exceptions are not subject to the rules of past experience — nor can they be easily answered from the weight of accumulated knowledge. Consultants can be misled on this point, however, because today, with knowledge so poorly organized and managers so confused, "exceptions" are quite easy to fix (because they arise from the manager's, and not society's, ignorance). But as expert programs codify knowledge and apply it where it normally belongs, the worker's ignorance dissipates. The worker is either completely replaced or has been "taught" by the software and now deals with anomalies in the workflow. The manager deals with the exceptions the worker cannot resolve, and the consultants deal with the exceptions the managers cannot resolve. At the consultant's level, these will be truly grand problems, fully worthy of the range and flexibility of the human mind (or team of minds, as will usually be the case). But consultants need to be ready for these new challenges, since their "easy" problems are about to be swept into history.

These changes will require consultants to define their relationship to software developers. While the smaller consultancies will usually be content to buy their software from competing vendors, many of the larger firms, afraid to rely too heavily on outside suppliers for products critical to their success, will push for collaborative relationships. They will understand that their customer knowledge is an indispensable part of the creation of many kinds of expert programs, and it will occur to them that they should share in the reward. There is also the inviting possibility that a tight relationship with a developer would result in a competitive advantage for one consultancy over others. The software developer, in turn, will see the consultancies as a source of information, cash, and distribution strength.

Computing consultants who are not part of broader firms will find themselves in an increasingly awkward position. Even though there is a continuing high demand for their services, they need to ask whether they see themselves as elite technicians, taking their instructions from others, or whether they wish to shape computing in their image. They need to compare the relative value of their technical expertise to the value of knowledge itself, or at least determine how society makes that judgement. And they must decide whether they are consultants or software developers, or both. If they try to do both, there is the risk they will do neither well. It may be that the computing consultancies will have to grow to a considerable size to hold their own in their relationships with clients, developers, and other consultants. However these relationships work out, it is quite clear that a computing consultancy that cannot command content will fail to achieve wide influence.

Clients also have some difficult changes to make as both computing and consulting provide a growing source of competitive advantage. In a world of expanding information, there is more to know than any organization can achieve in-house, and this is the foundation on which consulting will thrive. But clients will have to decide how dependent they should be on others for their most vital information. This debate is essentially about the division of power and profit. While the client cannot do it all, it is not clear exactly what should be delegated to the consultant and whether that delegation should happen on a continuing basis. Many clients are quite unprepared to make these decisions because they have no credible information strategy. Until they know what information they need, who needs it, how to find or create it, and how to save and apply it, they will not be able to use consultants effectively. In the future, a client who does not know how to make use of consultants will be as disadvantaged as a company that does not know how to deploy its capital.

ENDLESS PROBLEMS

All consultants, computing and otherwise, face a range of problems that is literally unbounded. Hence, the consultancies would in general be expected to welcome almost any kind of expert program. But in practice, they are essentially focused on some of the business community's most critical problems. Companies, after all, do not call consultants about the obstacles they easily master. In this sense, consultants are intimately involved with the most valuable applications of the expert system. Whether they recognize the commercial advantage of this is not exactly clear. Generally, consultants are concerned with the management of computer capabilities, human-resources management, organizational design, corporate strategy, and technology transfer. Each of these areas invites expert systems, and each system could build on the consultancy's competence in a marketplace where the customers have already asked for help. All of these areas are highly complex, with researchable and information-dependent solutions — the prerequisites of expert systems.

For example, an elite consulting practice might be tempted to use or develop an expert system to deal with the prolonged inability of an organization to achieve its goals, even while using expert systems of its own. The problem could be a hardware failure, a coding error, incorrect or corrupted data, a security breach, or a fundamental flaw in the algorithm. This is an ideal problem for yet another kind of expert system, a computerized sleuth. Once the problem is found and fixed, the solution will be subsumed into the relevant expert program. The answer will be computer downloaded — once.

THE RIGHT PERSON IN THE RIGHT JOB

Organizational failures may also be caused by an inappropriate program/human interface, or even by a worker who is misusing the system through ignorance or design. Thus human-resource management and organizational design offer attractive opportunities for both consultants and their expert systems. The computerization of the workplace is eliminating all routine work, not all workers. And the ability of organizations to deliver their products effectively is dependent on both the expert system and the remaining workers (through whose hands decisions and products still move). While some decisions will be implemented machine to machine, many others will be implemented by human agents for human agents.

Therefore, there will be situations in which the right information is still not being delivered to the right person, or it is being delivered with an unclear or ambiguous meaning. Because of the vagaries of human behaviour, it will be a challenge to avoid engaging in a wild goose chase through the innards of the computer system. And it will be equally difficult to identify the worker who receives the correct information but uses it incorrectly because of a limitation in understanding. Here the solution is education and evaluation.

Regrettably, there is the rare worker who knowingly sabotages an activity for personal advantage or caprice. These computer systems are vulnerable to great damage from the hardest-to-detect source, a source determined to cover his tracks. Security will, of course, be a continuing focus of consulting.

Consultants will often find that the root of the problem is that the individual is unsuited to the job function. This will mean the reassignment or departure of the individual, as well as a reappraisal of the organization's human-resources procedures. But if consultants are called in only when the problem is major, that probably means that the individual involved is a senior executive, or that an entire division has the wrong people in place. In the latter case, the basic human-resources policy must be in systemic failure. The consultants are now dealing with the most vital of an organization's functions: who leads it and how human talent is being managed.

When senior executives need to be reassigned, consultants will be happy to fill any gaps by drawing on their executive recruitment services, a large and lucrative aspect of their business. However, the recruitment of senior executives will soon be highly dependent on expert software (unlike today, when the personal network is pre-eminent). The experience of a seasoned recruiter, while not to be dismissed, will no longer be adequate, given the sophistication of the skills in demand and the tight supply. Effective recruitment will require both the talents of an experienced team and the full weight of scientific investigation and evidence (expressed in computerized form).

But because executive candidates will need to exhibit such broad and flexible experience, most consultancies will want to buy or create their own evaluation programs. The consultancies will use as a starting point the evaluation programs common to business and education. Many will exhaustively research every aspect of leadership, creating a proprietary database that will chart the career paths of thousands of executives and identify benchmarks associated with success or failure.

Of course, only a large market can bear the cost of this research, and the firms are likely to position it as part of their consulting services, not a discrete product. However, the work that goes into producing the "executive" expert system might be the foundation for specialized evaluation applications that serve a broader range of occupations. The consultancy would also perhaps be tempted to provide these broader systems as explicit software products. This would put them in competition with software firms offering similar products, although the "brand name" of the consultancy might be a significant marketing advantage. Whatever the case, the entire category of evaluation software can be expected to grow rapidly.

What happens, however, when a company's problems stem not from staffing issues but from the fact that the workflow and division of labour make it difficult or impossible for anyone to perform well? To solve this problem, consultants will use organizational simulation software. Such software may do no more than generate alternative workflows and workplace structures, with the consultants choosing the best alternative based on their experience. However, a fully developed expert simulator would use its judgement to recommend the structure it felt would be most effective. Because organizations can be structured in literally unlimited numbers of ways, an organizational simulation based on objective experience should be very helpful. At this high level of analysis, one of the consultant's prime responsibilities will be to override the program where justified.

SIFT THE TECHNOLOGY

The consulting practices and their expert systems will also tackle those fields that facilitate technology transfer. Competition will require technology to be moved to where it is needed at ever faster rates, and thus transfer effectiveness and efficiency will assume increasing importance. But even those who are using the most expert of search engines in the best organized databases will realize that it is often difficult to find what is needed, precisely because we do not know what to look for. And we do not know what to look for because we do not know what there is. This problem cannot be solved with existing approaches.

Companies that are searching for new technology can only guess what is available. They need some way to learn what is coming down the pike. If a company believes it needs a better way to shape metal parts, for example, how is it to know it really needs to replace the metal with a new plastic that was just introduced? On the other hand, suppliers of technology are never quite aware of all the potential uses for their products. To achieve this awareness, they would have to draw on the imagination of thousands of minds. They would also have to second-guess the marketplace, and we know the abysmal track record of central planners that tried to do just that.

The present strategies employed to identify useful technology can most charitably be described as expedient and crude. Networking, consultants, trade shows, and publications are employed by the searchers; advertising and every form of promotional gambit are used by the technology suppliers. This all barely works, and technology moves either by random luck or very slowly. This slow pace is inadequate to the rate at which opportunities, and dangers, are being generated.

Technology transfer merits a more logical approach, one that views the volume of available data as a promising panorama and not a nightmarish barrier. As we have discussed previously, expert software is usually a very targeted solution. Even an expert search engine is still too general for the transfer function, as it will not deal precisely enough with the complexities of transfer. Because technology transfer is so economically critical, it's easy to justify the creation of a more focused tool, a search engine specifically designed for transfer. This would involve several components. The transfer engine would have access to the expert rules for technology transfer by industry. These expert rules would have been created by an analysis of all transfer instances in the industry in question. The analysis would describe whether new technology was created in-house or outside, who the typical outsiders were, whether pure science drove the adopted technologies, what changes preceded the creation of the transfer technologies, what changes preceded the adoption of the technologies, what the personal characteristics of the creators and adapters of transferred technology were, how often the technology appeared "randomly," and so on. Despite the importance of transfer, the above observations are currently unavailable in any detail (except in a few rare cases).

The issues described above are so straightforward that they are well within the computer's current capacity to search, sort, match, and remember. Indeed, most business problems are, at a basic level, much more similar than they at first seem (a fact software companies would know if they studied the world of their principal customers). But many developers are beguiled by the complexities and details of implementation. The expert transfer program would look beyond the clutter and strike to the fundamentals.

Again, it must be noted that the transfer programs will not replace the consultant. However, the consultant will be free to deal with "higher order" (that is, more difficult) problems. These range from the appropriate use of the transfer program to the strategic implementation of results. And as always, the consultants will address the ongoing anomalies and exceptions.

GRAND STRATEGY

Of course, there are problems that have nothing to do with inappropriate tasks or unsuitable employees. These problems often represent a fundamental challenge to the organization's strategic direction or a persistent inability to generate a necessary innovation, and consultants will have three ways to respond.

If the problem is that the client is not using the best available expert systems, including those designed to aid strategy formulation and innovation, the consultancy may be able to provide its own "elite" strategy program. Strategy programs recommend solutions by drawing on thousands of examples of business, military, and political strategies; these programs are similar in structure to the organizational simulation programs. Guiding clients through the land of expert systems will become a critical function of most major consultancies.

If the consultant finds that the client's tools are only state of the art, it may be able to draw on experimental programs just beyond the leading edge. Often having this access to the latest of the new can mean a great competitive advantage. Alliances among the consultancies, the major software companies, and the non-profit research facilities would give the consultancies privileged access. The client will have to be advised that this approach carries with it more than normal risk, of course.

If existing software tools fail to solve the problem, consultants will serve as elite human experts, schooled and experienced as they are in the great exceptions of life. They will, of course, be part of a network of experts who will meet in person frequently. The elite only clean up details electronically; they think in each other's physical presence. Interestingly enough, these consulting experts will sometimes do no more than confirm the "extraordinary" judgement of the client's own executives. But the confirmation will be a truly valuable service. It will steel conviction and give courage to those who lack it, including the investors.

Since the consultancies will see themselves as the repository of special talent, they will have to redouble their own efforts to recruit and retain people of exceptional flexibility of mind and profound depth of knowledge. When everyone's work becomes more challenging, the standard of performance for those who want to stand at the apex of difficulty becomes Olympian. But this is what the marketplace will demand. If consultancies do not deliver this standard, they will fade. Already some feel themselves under pressure as computerized tools render some of their services unnecessary.

The consultancies that survive will have to track their talent for years, nurturing it with mentorships through several levels of education. Special apprenticeships will also be arranged with key clients. The consultancies will face so critical a need for overwhelming talent that they will intrude or assist in academic curriculum development. And certainly, they will move far beyond their traditional home turf, the business school. Fortunately, those chosen will demand money as only a partial incentive; they will also have to be offered opportunities for high satisfaction and major social or economic impact. Consultancies will also have to focus on generating the kind of clients for which their key employees want to work.

Almost all consultancies will treat computing talent as a vital component of their range of capabilities. This will result in some organizational stress as they try to decide how this talent relates to other capabilities. They will have to decide whether they are aggressive supporters of expert systems, or whether they will simply react to whatever comes along. While consultancies will certainly want to help select and implement expert software, they will struggle over whether they also want to develop it (either for their own use or for external sales). And they will face stiff competition from other consultants, from development companies, and from their clients. But there is no reason why the great class of advisers should face less competitive heat than their clients do.

•

CHAPTER TWELVE

INTO THE
TWENTY-FIRST CENTURY

JUST BEFORE THE DAWN

The Internet, cloning, fibre-optics, personal digital assistants, video downstreaming, high-definition television — all are technologies worthy of note. Yet the expert system, the technology that will shape *all* other technologies, remains in the shadows. Thus we face once again the classic situation where a powerful technology arises slowly and painfully, each small step attracting little attention. Then, as this disruptive technology reaches critical mass, it bursts into public view, apparently having been born overnight. The scramble to cope follows, with the small organization outperforming the big, as is so often the case. This accounts for the "sudden" appearance of the Internet and the panic it set off. And so it will be with expert systems, whose critical mass is almost upon us.

As expert systems are adopted, they will leave no structure or process untouched. Whether it's in scientific research, engineering design, marketing, finance, or human resources, the expert system will have its say. And most of the time, it will not be denied. By mobilizing knowledge and insisting on its use, these systems will produce a dramatic improvement in decision making. Given today's information chaos, nothing could be more critically important.

The effect of these systems is beyond question. While individual companies will try to use them to gain competitive advantage, the general level of competition will still continue to rise. The advance of technology, a factor that always increases competition, will now be accelerated by the expert systems themselves. The pace of change will be further increased because corporations will be able to respond to new opportunities and new competitive threats with a speed heretofore unimagined. Even corporations of considerable size will be able to change by literally reprogramming themselves. While it may take time to create the new instruction sets, these changes will be implemented with a speed that, by the standards of the past, seems almost instantaneous.

With the technological treadmill firmly in place, we run harder and harder to merely keep up with the herd. The economy will now start to move at the speed of the expert system. It will not be slowed to the lowest common denominator, which is the slowest employee's ability to adapt. The machinery now adapts and the organization responds. At the operational level of enterprise, one company's array of expert systems will be pitted against those of another company. As duelling software becomes normal practice, the world's game theorists will be overjoyed.

MAKE IT BETTER

At the strategic level, enterprise will have no choice but to seek advantage by creating innovation. In the business world of yesteryear, most companies had a few people whose jobs included some attempt at improvement or innovation. But the number of people and the total effort were relatively small compared with each company's need to manufacture and deliver its product or service. The expert systems rebalance this corporate allocation of resources. As they conduct more and more of the company's normal operations, the mandate to innovate grows. Those who monitor the expert systems that deliver the company's sales remain critically important, but they will be greatly outnumbered by those whose only job is to innovate.

The innovator's mandate is clear: find a way to improve the company's product or the way it is produced. Naturally enough, this will involve research, analysis, and experimentation — true knowledge work, creative and demanding, though the innovators will be aided by the expert systems for knowledge management and innovation. They will, of course, also have to draw on a wide array of human skills, from a knowledge of computing to an understanding of the intricacies of pure science. There will be those who creatively search for information, some who shape it into broad conceptual form, some who formulate detailed alternative answers, some who create the experiments, and some who implement the new answers (which usually appear as an improved expert system). In a company with a fully established set of expert systems, most employees will work on improvements; the rest will keep the expert systems working and substitute for them when they do not.

With the entire economy moving ever faster, innovations appearing more frequently, and smaller companies able to use expert systems to buy the "experience" of large and older enterprises, the competitive frenzy will be unprecedented. So, too, will the shift of power to the consumer. Many of today's companies will stumble on this point, some irretrievably. In the marketplace of the expert system, it will be more difficult to win, satisfy, and keep customers. And each dollar of profit will be harder won. From the customer's point of view, this means more choice, better service, and much better value — just as Adam Smith said would occur.

KNOWLEDGE IN CHARGE

Expert systems will force an unprecedented degree of change in both the conduct and the structure of business organizations. They cannot avoid producing these extraordinary effects, since they are redefining both the nature of work and the essence of management. No human organization will be immune, regardless of size or industry. Computerized expert systems will conduct, on a day-to-day basis, almost all of the traditional corporate functions, from human resources and financial control to production and marketing. Routine decision making will be embedded in the machinery.

The programmed corporation will fully recognize that its competitive advantage lies in its knowledge base. People may drive an organization, but information is both the destination and the means to get there. A company using expert systems can explicitly and aggressively decide what it knows, or should know, and how this information should be used.

The vendors of the expert systems will challenge all clients to become "knowledge corporations." And as corporations document their own knowledge, they will finally become fully aware of information in its various forms. They will finally understand how inadequately information is presently organized, how often it is wrong, and how easily it is lost or forgotten.

The claim, too often heard today, that "our people know" will sound hollow as the expert system reveals a multitude of decision-making defects. Therefore, even though these systems will be expensive, they will be worth it, if only because the anomalies they will eventually uncover are likely to be exacting a high cost on the organization.

BLESS THE LAWYERS

Of course, once the gaps are revealed, they cannot be left unaddressed. Ignorance of a problem is everyone's excuse for not having addressed it. But once you know that a problem exists, that knowledge serves as a moral rebuke, like an unwanted dinner guest waiting to be fed. And should management be tempted to declare the problem a low-level priority to be solved sometime in the future, there are two important obstacles. First, the process that identifies the problem does so by presenting it as part of the corporation's overall workflow. Therefore, its priority is simultaneously described, making it hard to shuffle the matter out of sight.

Second, documented gaps in procedure or knowledge are also fertile ground for litigation. The fiduciary responsibility of management to shareholders will often apply here. Ignoring a known problem that is critical to corporate function can appear to be an act of negligence. Gaps in decision making that affect worker or product safety are, of course, ripe areas for litigation. But many other kinds of business deficiencies can now become subject to litigation as well. The critical issue from the law's point of view would be that the problem was both known and could have been solved by established expert advice. As expert systems become the state of the art of management, it will be increasingly hard to explain their absence in this kind of legal proceeding. An aircraft that flies without its standard warning and fail-safe systems is too terrifying to be permitted. Corporations will soon find themselves in a similar position.

While there may be some debate about the extent to which a litigious environment serves society, legal threats will push expert systems even further into the realm of business. Courts will soon be asking, "What did he know, and when did he know it?" Soon, for the corporate world, expert systems will be giving evidence against their masters. The chain of accountability grows tighter and the evasion of truth becomes less possible.

LEADER/CREATOR

In a society where the routine becomes the responsibility of the computer, the role of the leader grows steadily in importance. Or does it? Not surprisingly, there are those who believe the computerization of the workplace will result in the hiring of only a handful of worker drones, with all the ultimate responsibility vested in the few at the top. It is an interesting fantasy, but one without foundation. First, there will be no drone workers because there will be no drone work. Second, the chief executives will not issue routine instructions, since that will be the responsibility of the machinery.

Whatever information flows to the executive suite will be meant only to generate non-routine instructions, to be creative, to seize unusual opportunities, to avert unexpected danger. In any large-scale organization, a few executives will be unequal to the task. There is too much to be absorbed and too many different ways to think about it.

So the responsibility for leadership widens. This can hardly be surprising when following is the job of the machine and the only work that remains is to lead. The chief executive becomes a leader of leaders, and in this way ensures that the whole company does not become obsolete in a single year. In other words, the world of work as created by expert systems will be an egalitarian society of those who used to be called executives. Everyone must lead, and the CEO is no more than first among equals. Rather than turning workers into human robots, expert systems must call forth human creators. The advance of expert systems challenges each of us to take a stand for or against the growth potential of the human species. That the transition from old work to new work will be traumatic is beyond doubt.

EYE OF THE HURRICANE

Fortunately, as expert systems take over an increasing share of a company's ongoing operations, the human workplace becomes less hectic, less a frenzy of people running in circles. A calmer atmosphere descends, one paced by the machinery's methodical chugging. Those who are monitoring the expert systems must watch vigilantly, however. It is not in the nature of the sentry to run randomly from post to post (or it should not be). And when on occasion a sentry must sound the alarm, it must be a clear voice echoing in the stillness of the night. It cannot be just one more shouted warning in a screaming crowd.

A quieter organization will also tend to be a more thoughtful one. Noise has always been the enemy of coherent thought. In this way, the age of information begins to have operational meaning. However, this more thoughtful corporation is not by any means a utopia. An environment that encourages thinking does not eliminate either error or the imperfections of human nature. Even well-meaning and reflective people can come to incorrect conclusions. Good scientists have led us down many a blind alley, remember. In fact, we have been collectively wrong about everything from the extinction of the dinosaurs to the essential elements of genetics. Moreover, thoughtfulness does not eliminate envy or fear, arrogance or prejudice, sloth or the lack of joy. If it did, then every university campus would be an Eden that no student would ever willingly leave.

But giving workers the time to think, inviting them to reflect and consider, does surely produce more thoughtful outcomes. It moderates the careless response and delivers new insights worthy of further exploration. In a few cases, a quiet moment of thought may even challenge those who treat others with disrespect to reconsider their behaviour. A thoughtful business environment, far from being the instant answer to all our problems, is just another important step forward in the conduct of human affairs.

CORPORATE CRUCIBLE

Even though the future is always a shifting array of possibilities driven by the self-fulfilling prophecies of those who dream, the course of expert systems can still be anticipated in broad terms. Since these systems will disrupt companies in virtually every way, great disasters await. We cannot expect anything else, given the bureaucratic slowness of all large organizations and the tendency for all of us to be trapped in the responses of yesterday. In the tumult that lies ahead, investors will rush to safe havens to save themselves from aerial bombardment. The foolish, by contrast, will jump on board every ill-conceived initiative just before it sinks out of sight. The gears of the overall marketplace will grind with stress as they shift forward into a world where knowledge really rules. The churn in the labour markets will frighten many into paralysis. As a result, expert systems will be resisted, denounced, tried, discontinued, and tried again. But because they work, they will finally triumph. Keeping one's eye on the distant horizon in the midst of this bedlam will be the greatest challenge of all.

PROMISE AHEAD

Yet as much *because* of the confusion as in spite of it, great opportunity awaits. Entire fields of endeavour are already waiting for the impulse to innovate. Indeed, this is the only work worthy of humans — to deal with the exceptional, to create wondrous works. While we will all have expert companions, the struggle will be ours as we rise to this higher standard of work.

Of course, this assumes that the potential of human ingenuity is realized only with very hard work. It is on this radical idea that the future of computing rests. Some may see this forecast as too demanding of human adaptability, if not too harsh. And that view may be quite fair, given that the marketplace is not known for its sensitivity to human feelings. But in the face of the pain, distress, and waste that are the products of our ignorance, a "forced march" towards enlightenment appears overdue.

In a world of knowledge, proprietary control of that knowledge through patents, copyright, and trade secrets is the commercial world's most important source of power. Indeed, many companies will create innovations that enjoy strong proprietary protection, monopoly profits, and extraordinary rates of return. These protections will diminish competition in some areas of the marketplace and heighten it in others (especially areas where the patent or copyright protects the young from the old, the small from the large).

The software industry will be affected in the same ways and to at least the same degree. As in other industries, some dominant players will be undermined and others will be strengthened. While the larger firms can bear both the cost and the risk of genuine information research more easily, they are also more likely to have difficulty moving beyond the responses that made them so successful in the past. Smaller firms may be more willing to adapt, even as they struggle to fund themselves. It will be interesting to see whether venture capital companies, whose mandate is the discovery of new commercial opportunities, will live up to their billing.

The only significant uncertainty appears to be how long it will take for expert systems to become dominant. The time horizon is, of course, critical to the foundation of empire or the genesis of decline. But it is clear enough that once expert software has reached a wide market, the lure of monopoly profits will cause a stampede of new entrants.

While expert software seems inevitable, the exact and immediate future is still what we choose it to be. But given the difficulty involved in creating this defining expression of software, there is no guarantee the opportunity will be quickly realized. As with all great enterprises, it will take individuals of passion and courage, the number of which is always open to question.

ACKNOWLEDGEMENTS

This book owes its creation to countless conversations with more people than can be named. I owe a great debt to the business community with which I have long been associated, and in particular to those who practise the art of information technology. Whether or not we agree in philosophy and approach, we all understand what an opportunity we have been given to help shape one of the planet's great technologies. I am especially grateful to those men and women who have had the courage, drive, and vision to create new ventures and innovative technologies. What I have learned from them is beyond measure, and I salute them as true pioneers.

I especially appreciate the support of my colleagues in the Department of Economics at the University of Waterloo, who understand my need to work in the private sector and who continue to invite me to teach. Above all, these gifted persons make me think. So, too, do faculties across the campus, who patiently offer guidance as I intrude into their technological domains. The welcome of the Faculty of Engineering has been particularly warm and entirely unreserved. In addition, I have valued my association with the Richard Ivey School of Business at the University of Western Ontario.

Nevertheless, the greatest contribution to this book has come from my students. By now more than 10,000 strong, these talented and accomplished men and women work in every one of North America's leading technological corporations, and in hundreds of start-ups. In conversations after class that extended late into the night, they both made me feel useful and humbled me by what they already knew. For the past twenty years, my students have briefed me on every major advance in information technology, before my colleagues in business were discussing it, before it was reported in the press. I soon made sure I listened. And after years of discussion and debate with these students, present and former, the main argument of this book came into view, and then they helped to refine it. For their advice and support, I am grateful beyond words.

I am pleased to acknowledge the help of Stoddart Publishing: Angel Guerra who told me to write the book I believe in, Don Bastian who patiently walked me through the process, and David Kilgour whose suggested changes made the manuscript stronger. Janice Weaver then helped me appear literate. And a special thank you is owed to Dan Komorowski, who brought the book to their attention.

Finally, I deeply appreciate ongoing administrative support without which I cannot function. Pat Shaw's care and concern for our students make it possible for me to remain in the classroom, and besides, she prepared the original manuscript. Carolyn Holden managed both me and the manuscript through to its completion. Without her good cheer, meticulous attention to detail, unfailing commitment, and eye for clarity in language, the manuscript would not have been delivered.

INDEX